Greiner

Racing Cars
AND THE
History of Motor Sport

Racing Cars
AND THE
History of Motor Sport

by PETER ROBERTS

Octopus Books

First published 1973 by
Octopus Books Limited
59 Grosvenor Street, London W.1.

ISBN 0 7064 0228 6

© 1973 Octopus Books Limited

Distributed in Australia by
Rigby Limited
30 North Terrace, Kent Town,
Adelaide, South Australia 5067

Produced by Mandarin Publishers Limited
14 Westlands Road, Quarry Bay, Hong Kong

Printed in Hong Kong

Contents

Chapter 1

The First Automobile Contest

Paris–Rouen 1894

Of course it was inevitable. And it was obvious to all who had the smallest interest in the new self-propelled vehicles that sooner or later some enterprising enthusiast would claim to be able to conduct his vehicle faster, or more reliably, or over a longer distance, or up a steeper hill, or rougher terrain, than the next horseless carriage enthusiast. By June 1894 it had started — the first of the long, heart-stopping, ever faster, tragedy-splashed sequence of motor sport events.

Pierre Giffard, energetic *Chef des Informations* of the Paris newspaper *Le Petit Journal*, had already sponsored a cycle race from Paris to Brest on the west coast of France and back, and had found that the publicity derived from the venture had boosted the sales of his paper. The automobile had been making its shaky progression for just nine years, and had not yet provided serious competition for a mule, let alone a carriage-and-pair or even a bicycle.

But the tempo of life was already beginning to accelerate in the late nineteenth century. And time was money to no one more than a newspaper editor. A crime had been committed in St. Denis, a few miles away from Giffard's office. The paper was about to be put to bed. Giffard needed this item to fill a corner, but time pressed. Perhaps his good friend Emile Levassor could take him out to St. Denis in that horseless

Early Peugeot. This vis-à-vis, with its 2 cylinder motor developing 15 h.p. was the type in which Armand Peugeot followed the cycle race from Paris to Brest and back in 1891.

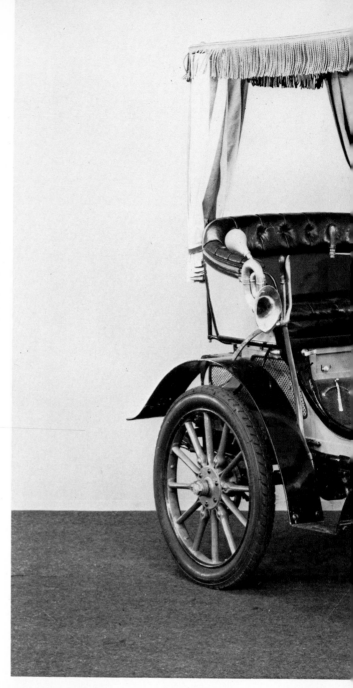

contraption of his with the German motor? No,
Levassor was away.

History does not record whether Giffard secured his
news item, but it certainly takes notice of the idea that
his dilemma generated. That evening in a Montmartre
cafe he put it to a colleague, Jacques Andrée. One of
the great nuisances about the new carriages was their
unpredictability, so why not organize a *Concours de
Voitures sans Chevaux*, a trial of reliability, from
Paris to Rouen? At least it would encourage the
tinkering owners to pay some attention to arriving at a
destination in one piece and, by happy chance, no
doubt boost circulation.

So *Le Petit Journal* (Tous les Jours, 5 centimes, with
illustrated supplement on Sundays) raised the necessary cash to get motor sport's first meeting off the
ground; the date, 22 July 1894. It was not a race—
officially—and the regulations stated that the winner
would be the vehicle that was: (1) without danger;
(2) easily handled by the drivers; (3) of low running
costs. *Le Petit Journal* would award 5,000 francs to the
winner of the 75 mile event.

On the cobbles of the Porte Maillot in Paris on that
Sunday morning assembled a strange assortment of
shivering, clanking vehicles. For the large crowd who
came to watch—and laugh—there was plenty of

entertainment. Of 102 entrants only 21 had arrived, although no doubt the immediate environs of Paris would have yielded a fine crop of smoking cripples. The military had come to see what could be in it for them; a sprinkling of technically-orientated people wandered around gleaning information, and several society ladies were there to show their new hats and to peer into the works. Even Gottlieb Daimler had come to see the fun. The sensible Württemberger had travelled to Paris by train, but Daimler had a special interest, of course. Most of the petrol-driven vehicles employed his engines or ones built under his licence. Five Peugeots and four Panhards, for instance, were propelled by Daimler-type 3 or 4 h.p. engines.

In the line-up were several steam vehicles; one, the first to arrive at Rouen later, a De Dion-Bouton that was eventually dropped down to second place because of its running costs, employed a stoker (chauffeur) on board as well as a driver. Other steamers contesting were a La Blant (which Etienne La Blant took up over the pavement, demolishing a public seat or two and causing a few ladies to have the vapours, even before the event started), a Serpollet and a large Scotte omnibus which, touchingly, was awarded a prize for the most enterprising vehicle *not* to finish.

The other 80 or so vehicles, the ones that didn't make the chalked-out start line, would have provided a much more unconventional array of engineering enterprise. Propellants such as steam and petrol were old-hat to some of these pioneers; gravity, the weight of the passengers, compressed air, large pendulums, and even a 'combination of mechanical and animate power' were employed to move, hopefully, these gems of impracticable ingenuity. Sadly not one remains.

Below top
The de Dion-Bouton steamer
entered in the Paris-Rouen
trials, without its tractor. This
car was first home, but was
awarded second place as it
employed a stoker.

Below centre
Three years before the 1894
contest Emile Levassor had
established his front-engined
design.

The start at 30-second intervals must have produced a memorable scene as spindly petrol vehicles set off down the road and steamers puffed along shrouded in their own excess. After the departure of the last hesitant steamer, Giffard and his colleagues entrained for Rouen.

Mishaps were not serious, although the reliability trial soon developed into a race—'Such is the competitive nature of the internal combustion engine that whoever conducts it along the highway must keep a firm rein to prevent it bolting,' said one contemporary observer in a rather backhanded way—and the Paris–Rouen competitors had hardly had a chance to learn the basic rules. A reporter from the New York Herald had been dispatched on a bicycle to write a running commentary, keeping up with the competitors. This he did without recording any difficulty.

As vehicles collapsed under the strain, the gallant survivors halted and picked up casualties. One patch of gravel just outside Les Andelys caused stones to lodge in the De Dion-Bouton spokes, delaying it for a time, while cursing passengers winkled them out again. A Bollée tried to take the loose patch at speed, and committed suicide right there. More vehicles fell *hors de combat* as the hours passed, and as the ancient city of Rouen appeared on the horizon the De Dion steamer led, followed by four petrol-driven carriages. The National Guard were out in force and dense crowds lined the streets. The competitors entered Rouen to the wild acclaim usually accorded to conquering heroes, which in a way, they were.

The De Dion tractor-and-trailer made the trip in the shortest time, averaging 11.6 m.p.h., and the two following Peugeots clocked in with an average of 11.5 and 11.1 m.p.h. Fourth was a Panhard and fifth

Right
Maurice La Blant's steam
omnibus, with room for nine
aboard; this vehicle trundled
along the Paris to Rouen road
picking up competitors whose
cars had broken down.

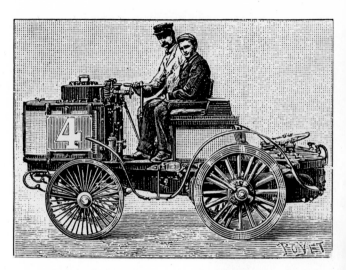

another Peugeot. But speed was not the official
criterion, and the first prize was eventually split
between Peugeot and Panhard as the most economic
and reliable vehicles to finish.

What had this first motor sport event achieved? The
Paris-Rouen trial both aroused public interest in the
motor vehicle itself and proved beyond any doubt that
it was the major means of transport for the future. The
event also minted the world 'automobile'. One other
thing was obvious; the French motoring community
couldn't wait to mount another event.

Chapter 2

Next Year,
Once Again

Paris–Bordeaux 1895

Eleven months after the Paris-Rouen Trial the French were at it again. This time it was to be a real race on public roads, from Paris to Bordeaux and back, a staggering distance of 732 miles. Three days were allowed for the distance and the route ran from the Place d'Armes at Versailles, through the Valley of Chevreuse, Limours, Etampes, Orléans, Tours, and then via the Route Nationale 10 to Bordeaux, returning by the same route.

This, the first genuine motor vehicle race, gave birth to a dozen different aspects of the sport, but is remembered more particularly for the astonishing endurance of Emile Levassor, who drove one of his own cars (a Panhard-Levassor) over the entire course, although the regulations stated that the driver could be changed, and arrived first at the finish, over 48 hours after starting. The drama of this unrepeatable feat is dimmed a little only when one learns that his average speed was around 15 m.p.h.

Again a variegated assembly of vehicles entered the lists. As the programme said, 46 vehicles engaged, 22 departed; including 12 voitures à pétrole, 6 voitures à vapeur, 1 électrique, 3 cycles à pétrole. One of the smaller Peugeots was driven by André and Edouard Michelin, who had been making pneumatic bicycle tyres for some time and were now trying them out on

No. 5, Emile Levassor's car, at the Place d'Armes at Versailles before the start of the epic Paris-Bordeaux-Paris race. Levassor won (unofficially) the 732 mile race, driving the entire distance himself.

12

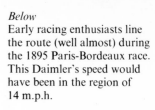

Below
Early racing enthusiasts line
the route (well almost) during
the 1895 Paris-Bordeaux race.
This Daimler's speed would
have been in the region of
14 m.p.h.

an automobile under battle conditions. One large steam bus by Bollée, was so sophisticated that it had its own toilette—the seven passengers it carried on the race probably needed it, so rough and bumpy was the French pavé.

Levassor's car was a two-seater, powered as usual by a Daimler unit of 4 h.p. He knew that he would be barred from receiving an award even if he won, as the (admittedly rather sketchy) regulations laid down that competing vehicles should have at least four seats. And he did win, a great single-handed feat unique in motoring history.

Emile Levassor got away from the Versailles start line around midday, headed south-west towards Bordeaux, and did so well over the 366 miles of rough and dusty roads that he arrived at Bordeaux about 10.10 a.m. on the following day. Passing Ruffec, the town on the route where his No. 2 driver had been waiting to take over the wheel, Levassor had been so well ahead of schedule (he arrived in the small hours of

the night when his relief was still abed) that he decided to drive on to Bordeaux himself. On the return leg he passed through Ruffec again and this time his No. 2 was awake and ready to take over. However, the 52 year-old car manufacturer had by now caught a strong dose of racing fever and opted to carry on at the wheel.

Somewhere on the way back—during the second evening of the race—Levassor met the other competitors clanking along the road towards Bordeaux. His car was still running perfectly, although he had hit a plank he had left in the road after his lighting system had fallen off.

The first to cross the line at Paris—almost six hours ahead of his closest rival—Levassor and his Panhard were feted, and then disqualified. But a moral victory was won by the French driver, and it is he who is remembered when they talk of those heroic first days of motor sport and of the endurance of men at the wheel. Nearly 50 hours at what were then racing speeds—and all on a glass or two of Champagne at Bordeaux, and a couple of poached eggs with a bowl of soup at the finish.

Thus the marathon motor race was born, the racing hero entered history and sports vehicles (two-seater variety) took shape. And this first race also proved another point. Petrol engines were more reliable than steam; nine of the first ten cars home were driven by internal combustion motors.

Meanwhile, Back In The USA

Times Herald Race 1895

Reports of the 1894 Paris-Rouen competition soon crossed the Atlantic, and during the autumn of that year a young journalist working for the Chicago Times Herald managed to sell his boss the idea of setting up a race in the United States, and donating $5,000 to it.

The response was tremendous. Nearly a hundred backyard builders entered as contestants. H. H. Kohlsatt, editor of the Times Herald, was overjoyed at the coming publicity for his paper. His enthusiasm waned as the day of the race drew nearer and all but two of the 'entrants' fell out. Their cars may have been built in their heads but had not, up to then, taken physical shape. The race was postponed until November 1895.

On a slushy, slippery day—so miserable that the race was shortened from 94 to 54 miles—six cars slid about on the Chicago start line, waiting to make their dash to Evanston. A couple of electrics sat silently there while a Duryea, two Benz, and a Roger-Benz huffed and puffed and warmed their innards.

All but two cars ended as roadside furniture, Oscar Muller's Benz and Frank Duryea's car being the lone survivors. Duryea did the run, according to many historians, in 8 hours 23 minutes, and Muller arrived at the finish 1 hour 35 minutes later. In fact, the situation is historically rather hazy; German reports tend to favour the Benz as winner, American writers the Duryea. It is also written that Muller collapsed with fatigue and was not at the wheel for the last part of the event, and that his travelling umpire Charles King (of later fame) drove the Benz over the last miles. One of the most authoritative British record books, the *Guinness Book of Car Facts and Feats* records that the 2 cylinder Duryea won. Another British author states that everyone was disqualified anyway (the sport was always thus troubled with the interpretation of regulations) and that nobody won, but that prizes were given to almost everybody within shouting distance.

Whatever the result, the Times-Herald race, the first in the United States, opened the gates to the age of motor sport in that great country.

A Benz Victoria of 1893. Karl Benz, conservative in many ways recognized the value of competition success and entered his cars in many early events.

Chapter 3

Europe Moves On

The Growing Giants

Now France, as virtually the only European nation with both the means and experience to organize motor competitions, was aflame with enthusiasm (although the flames were confined to those who actually knew what an automobile was) and motor racing quickly slipped into gear.

The Automobile Club de France had been formed in 1895, and with typical French élan it organized another marathon, this time the almost incredible distance of 1,711 kilometres, from Paris to Marseilles in the south of France and back again. For this 10 days were allowed—a pattern that was to become normal in the long road races to come, and one that was in fact a blueprint for rallying.

Other races were fought out that year; Bordeaux—Langon, Bordeaux—Agen—Bordeaux (could it have been that the exploits of M. Levassor had fired the Bordelaise?), a *course handicap* at Spa in Belgium mounted by the new Automobile Club de Belgique. It was beginning to spread like a . . . well, it depended on your viewpoint.

In 1897 the big event was a comparatively short one, a race from Marseilles through Nice to the village of La Turbie, high above the Principality of Monaco. Short it may have been but it demanded a new technique, that of climbing steep hills with their sharp corners at

By the turn of the century motor sport had become fashionable, and races proliferated. Here the driver of a large 1901 Mors waits for the start-signal (a hand-held newspaper!) to send him scorching down the dusty highway.

Left
The Paris-Amsterdam-Paris event signalled the start of international racing on 7 July 1898. A full week was allowed for the course.

Below
The first significant motor sport event in Britain was the Thousand Miles Reliability Trial, a London-to-Edinburgh-and-back safari. Here a de Dion voiturette returns to London.

Right
The twentieth century car arrives. The first Mercedes, named after the 11-year-old daughter of Daimler's French representative, jolted the automobile world.

Bottom right
The Bordeaux to Agen race of 1898 was another event. Luckier than the British sports enthusiasts in France were allowed to use the open roads for speed events.

speed. Next year motor racing became international with the Paris-Amsterdam-Paris event.

As the racing became tougher, longer, more sophisticated, so the cars were changing. In 1895 Levassor's Panhard had been a road vehicle designed specifically to carry two people, and developed about 4 h.p. By 1898 Charron's winning Amsterdam Panhard (race-average nearly 30 m.p.h.) was a four-cylinder car of 2.4 litres, and a 4.5 litre model was made the following year. Thus, to keep the rapidly growing monsters at bay, and to attract less expensive vehicles, voiturette racing was born, a class which, at first, limited weight to between 200 and 400 kilogrammes.

A *Tour de France* for motor vehicles in 1899 was supported by a crop of smaller events from Paris to St. Malo, Trouville, Ostend, Biarritz, Rambouillet, and even one bizarre event in which the automobile was matched against a horse. The horse won.

But the monsters were still growing, now faster than ever. By 1900 a frightening Panhard of 7 litres appeared, only to be topped by a Mors of 10 litres capacity. Clumsy, sharp-edged things they were, wood-framed, with cast-iron works, constant-speed engines; products of their century but, to be fair, representing an astonishingly rapid advance in performance, if not in design. Then, in 1901, the twentieth century car arrived, the German Daimler with a young girl's name—Mercedes.

Nice Week of 1901 saw Mercedes driver Werner a treble winner, but later in the year first place in the Paris-Berlin race fell to a French car—so did second, third, fourth . . . right down the line to sixteenth. Werner, in the first Mercedes, was seventeenth.

Five years before the Paris-Berlin event, the British Lion had opened an eye, observed that motoring appeared to be here to stay, at least for a while, and had unshackled the British motorist by raising the speed limit from 4 m.p.h., plus a man-to-walk-in-front, to 12 m.p.h., but forbade road racing on the mainland. Not until 1900 were both eyes opened, to allow the most significant motoring event of the Victorian era to take place, the Thousand Mile Reliability Trial. This was a fairly leisurely London to Edinburgh and back, hock-and-sandwich trip, that demonstrated the potential of the motor car to the British public—as often as not for the first time.

Chapter 4

Small Car Victory

Paris–Vienna 1902

The time 8 p.m. The date 24 June 1902, the place, Paris. The city is *en fête* and the streets in the warm evening air are sparkling with coloured lights and crowded with festive citizens. The cafés of the Left Bank have been doing fine trade, and now the crowd gradually drifts to horse-omnibus stops, cab ranks, and the railway station. All travel to Champigny (over 10,000 of them) to see the start of the Race of Races, due to commence at 3.30 a.m., an hour before dawn.

And this really *was* a race—over 1,050 miles of rough roads through France, Switzerland, the Austrian Tyrol, crossing the mighty, cloud-hidden Arlberg Pass, and on to the city of the Danube and Strauss. To be run concurrently and within this daunting Paris-Vienna event was the second of the Gordon Bennett Cup races, which was to end at Innsbruck.

Bennett, proprietor of the New York Herald, the paper that had sent a reporter to the 1894 Paris-Rouen Trial, had shown a keen interest in the new sport and had mounted his first event in 1900, a race from Paris to Lyons. It had been chaotic, partly because of its 1,000 kg maximum weight restriction, and regulations which allowed each country to enter only three cars, all parts of which had to be manufactured nationally. Only five cars turned up for the first Gordon Bennett race and just two finished—

1902, the Paris-Vienna race.
Marcel Renault at the Belfort
check point before going on to
win the event.

Tous les Véhicules, gros et petits

de la Course

PARIS - VIENNE

sont battus par la

VOITURE LÉGÈRE

RENAULT Frères

montée par

Marcel RENAULT

1er du Classement Général
1er de toutes les Catégories

grâce à sa Voiture Légère RENAULT Frères à

Moteur 4 Cylindres

RENAULT Frères

qui pour ses débuts s'affirme SUPÉRIEUR à
tout ce qui s'est fait à ce jour !

24

Charron and Girardot on Panhard-Levassors. Said a contemporary writer: 'The organization was extremely poor, Charron having to get down from his car very often to ask his way . . . and just at the finish an enormous dog jumped between the right front wheel and the spring, and the car instantly ran off the road, went between two trees, and after sixty yards of wild running was steered again on to the road.' If this sort of thing happened to the winner one may imagine the disasters that befell the rest of the field.

The 1902 Paris-Vienna race would fill a book with near-incredible incidents, for instance the driver who sawed up the legs of a hotel table on one of the night halts, and smuggled them out to the yard where he trimmed them down for spokes. Another driver, a Captain Genty, cruising happily downhill in his Clément, heard shouts of distress behind him from

Right
British driver Charles Jarrot arrives at the Belfort control. He reported an uneventful run, but complained of the blinding dust which prevented him passing other competitors . . .

Below
. . . and an artist's view of the same car and driver in a later race.

Far right
Two minutes after mid-day, and Marcel Renault arrives in Vienna, so far ahead of schedule that little had been prepared for the victor—just a couple of early photographers and the odd top-hatted official.

a runaway motor-cyclist who was fast catching him up. As the unfortunate two-wheeler rattled past the Clément, the gallant captain hauled the rider safely aboard by the scruff of his neck . . . and other odd tales.

Forecasting the hazards of the event, two were described by a magazine thus: 'Among the excitements of a race which will provide a thrill at every corner, not the least startling experiences will be the jumping of the hundreds of caviveaux, or cross channels which, like miniature fords cross the road and scar bridges, colloquially known as donkey-backs, which, with a steep run up, endue a fast car with powers of aerial flight for a brief moment, and the descent may or may not be on the road.'

Promptly at 3.30 a.m. on 25 July 1902 the first of the 117 cars set off in a cloud of dust which enveloped most

of the 50,000 spectators that had by now gathered on Champigny Hill. First the Gordon Bennett cars departed; Girardot in his CGV; two minutes later, Fournier in a 60 h.p. Mors, British driver S. F. Edge in a Napier, and the Chevalier René de Knyff, conducting a 70 h.p. Panhard.

The race was run in four stages, Paris to Belfort near the Swiss border, Belfort to Bregenz (this stage through Switzerland had been 'neutralized' so that the cars went through as tourists), Bregenz to Salzburg, and finally Salzburg to Vienna, a total *racing* distance of 695½ miles.

At this time the upper weight limit was 1,000 kgs, and many of the larger vehicles had been lightened by paring back their superstructure and cutting down frames to a risky minimum. In addition, some manu-

facturers had actually increased the size of the engines and put them into these lighter frames. However, others, notably Renault, had entered small four-cylinder cars developing about 30 h.p. in the hope that the heavier cars would break up on the atrocious roads of Austria—which about half of them did.

The first day out was a Fournier gala. The route followed a railway line for part of the way to Belfort and a special express train carrying fans to the finish of the first stage enabled them to watch the race in progress. They were in a frenzy of enthusiasm, especially when the French Mors driver gave them a bonus by passing and re-passing the train. He dropped out shortly after these theatricals with a broken gear-box. Chevalier de Knyff entered Belfort in the lead, followed by five large Panhards. But they had been

travelling on good straight roads where they could use their power; the mountain sections were to come . . .

The Swiss section was taken in strict order at touring speed. Sensible in those days, as Swiss mountain passes had not been greatly improved since the days when Roman Legions crossed them.

The race was resumed the next day, when the survivors had the Arlberg ahead. This had been blocked by snow until a few days previously, but had been cleared—more or less. This is how S. F. Edge described part of the 6,000 ft. Alpine pass: 'The ascent and descent was an awful experience. The road curved and twisted interminably, and continually turned on itself, until at one moment the driver was gazing down the road he had passed along a few minutes pre-viously. Some of the gradients were so steep that they seemed to be almost perpendicular. Slipping about on the loose stones there was nothing to save the car from going down the side of the mountain in the event of a mistake in steering . . . the driver did not dare take his hands off the steering wheel.'

On this first Austrian stage the roads were in places so rough and time so pressing that some drivers lashed their feet to the pedals so that they could not be catapulted from their car at speed. Some of the hills were so steep that several competitors turned their cars round, and put them up the slope in reverse gear as the ratio was slightly lower. The entire route was littered with jettisoned toolboxes, oilcans, umbrellas and canvas coverings to lighten the vehicles.

Just after Bregenz Edge's Gordon Bennett Napier slid off the road into a ditch, and he lost vital minutes. Later, on the far side of the Arlberg he saw the Chevalier de Knyff, who had been the favourite for the Gordon Bennett Trophy, at the side of the road with a shattered differential, and resignation turned to elation as he realized he was in the lead. British visitors had a great day when it was learned that the Napier had won the Paris to Innsbruck event.

Meanwhile the rest of the field roared and skidded on towards Salzburg, birthplace of Mozart. Here young Marcel Renault entered the scene in the new 4 cylinder light car with the alligator bonnet. The medieval roads of the Alpine regions had broken the backs of so many of the big boys that Marcel entered Salzburg a creditable seventh, his brother Louis lying way back at sixty-first. A tough 40 h.p. Mercedes won the stage.

The last trek was to Vienna on a fairly good road. Almost every car left in the race was damaged and the result was still in the lap of the gods. Marcel Renault's machine, which had, in his own words, crossed the Arlberg 'as though it had wings' plunged down the Vienna road at over 70 m.p.h., taking corners at nerve-shredding speeds in a final gamble. He slowly cut down the distance between the Renault and Farman's big Panhard, passing Edmond's Darracq after a battle in which Renault was forced to drive blindly into the other's dust-cloud—losing his left wing in the process.

Then he took Count Zborowski's Mercedes, still aiming at catching Farman. Creeping up, the Renault began to catch the Panhard on the corners, the bigger car widening the gap on the frequent straights. Marcel finally passed the Panhard on a sharp country corner, and the road was his.

In Vienna, officials had forecast a 2 p.m. arrival. The little Renault appeared at the end of the Prater at just two minutes past midday. Nobody was ready for him. No route markers showed the way to the finish, no officials directed the winning car. Hawkers still sold their wares, the crowds were still more interested in a Sunday afternoon drink than in the race's first arrival. Renault's small red car had difficulty in getting through the crowds packing the Prater—everybody thought he was a gatecrasher. 'It is I, Marcel Renault,' he shouted to them, 'I have come from Paris!' Slowly it dawned on the assembly that here was the winner of the race, the greatest race of them all, and it was a *Frenchman*. Astonishment and disappointment mingled. Where were the Mercedes? Where was Zborowski? The military band hurriedly leafed over its music, found the *Marseillaise* and oompahed it out to the throng. When Farman made it a double French win, stupefaction set in. But the glory firmly belonged to Marcel Renault in his little automobile.

That race was won at an overall speed of 39 m.p.h., in seven hours less than the famous Arlberg Express train could cover the distance. It focused attention on light cars, and it encouraged manufacturers to produce them. What it did for the company of Renault Frères can be left to the imagination.

Paris-Madrid 1903

The inter-capital races had now engendered a fever of competition motoring, and in 1903 the racing world mounted an even bigger event, from Paris to Madrid. There were no less than 250 cars entered—the entire motor competition world—including several formidable works teams. Over 100,000 spectators assembled to see them off from Versailles, and the leaders were battling for prime place before the race was a few minutes old. The Renault brothers, Louis and Marcel, decided to get up in front to avoid the blinding dust

raised by the field, and pushed ahead at over 80 m.p.h. —a horrifying speed over rutted and pitted roads.

Louis took the lead, but behind him the first of several tragedies was being enacted. By the end of the first stage only 100 cars had survived, leaving a trail of broken vehicles and despondent or injured drivers. But far worse, the race had already killed 10 people, spectators and drivers, including Marcel Renault, who had taken a corner too fast through a cloud of dust, spun and crashed. Louis Renault withdrew his cars as soon as he heard of the death of his brother, but the Government went further and stopped the race, insisting that the cars should return home by rail.

So, in that sad sprint of 1903 ended the fantastic capital-to-capital races of early motoring days.

Chapter 5

Racing In The USA

Vanderbilt Cup Days

W. K. Vanderbilt had been interested in horses, motor-boats, and the automobile. As one of the richest men in America he bought only the best and in the early 1900s that, in terms of road transport, was a 70 h.p. Mors.

Willie K, fired by his own exploits in races such as the great international events that culminated in the disaster of the 1903 Paris-Madrid race, offered a valuable trophy for a series of races to be held in the United States. 'To encourage the development of the automobile in this country,' as he put it, knowing full well of the superiority of European machinery then.

The course for the first Vanderbilt Cup was on Long Island (a later race actually ran through New York City, at Queens) and was scheduled for 18 October 1904. Although, officially, subsequent races should have been held in the country of the previous year's victor, like the Gordon Bennett Cup, they were in fact all run in the USA from 1904 to 1916.

The first Vanderbilt Cup was all too exciting. It was, after all, the first real fast competition ever held in the United States, precursor of the American Grand Prize (which was set up as a counter-attraction, accepting cars of unlimited capacity, in contrast to the limits of 4,993 c.c. to 9,832 c.c. of the Vanderbilt Cup entrants) and of course of every other race in the country. And

Felice Nazzaro in the 110 h.p. Fiat at the start of the 1905 Vanderbilt Cup at Long Island. This, the second of the series, was won by Victor Hémery in a Darracq.

START AND FIN

Left
The American Grand Prize, organized by the Automobile Club of America, finally stole the Vanderbilt thunder and captured the big crowds. This is Hémery in a Benz re-fuelling at the 1910 race.

Below left
The 1912 Grand Prize of America. This year it was moved to a road circuit in Milwaukee. The winner, Teddy Tetzlaff (No. 20) can just be seen through the dust.

Right
Just before the New York 24 race of 1909 starts, Raffalovich, driver of Renault No. 1 fits his 'secret weapon'—mudguards— to his car. These, he hoped, would save him from the very real danger of flying stones.

Below
Vanderbilt Cup, 1906. A de Dietrich churns through a fast rough bend at Long Island . . .

. . . followed by Italian driver Alessandro Cagno in an Itala.

America loved it. The sight of Werner's 90 h.p. Mercedes, a 60 h.p. Renault, three Panhards, two Pope-Toledos, a Simplex and a Packard Grey Wolf was guaranteed to hold any red-blooded American auto fan mesmerized for the day. But the 30,000 spectators lining the route had about as much knowledge of motor racing speeds as the French crowds who had earlier watched the Paris races, and caused as much chaos. However the real trouble was the lack of even the most primitive safety barriers—and the shouted warning, 'Car coming!' saved many a spectator from a sticky end. As it was dozens of them dived for ditches as the speeding cars swept past them like maniac snowploughs. And what with drivers getting stuck in trolley lines, engines falling out of frames, over-drilled chassis buckling at speed, suspensions and brakes packing up due to half-a-dozen washboard level crossings on the course and a certain amount of blood, the crowds were well satisfied that October day in 1904.

Tragedy almost visited the race—once the winner George Heath in a Panhard (with a respectable 52.2 m.p.h. average) passed the post, the nearby crowd thought all was over and swarmed onto the track. Officials hurriedly stopped the rest of the field in an attempt to avoid a massacre.

The Vanderbilt Cup in those early years of the century did a great deal for American automobilism and for the industry, to say nothing of being the biggest automotive social event in the calendar—it even had a Broadway musical named after it. The 1906 race, for instance, attracted around a quarter of a million watchers (a larger crowd than attends most modern Grands Prix) all out for a Derby day outing on Long Island.

The American Grand Prizes organized by the Automobile Club of America, finally stole the Vanderbilt thunder and the first one captured most of the top pilots such as Nazarro, Wagner and Hémery. In its last four or five years the Vanderbilt Cup moved about the country in an effort to retain interest. The race, or at least its name, was revived for two years in 1936–7 at Roosevelt Raceway, where the distinguished racing drivers Nuvolari and Rosemeyer won the event.

Vanderbilt Cup Winners

1904	G. Heath	Panhard	Long Island
1905	V. Hémery	Darracq	Long Island
1906	I. Wagner	Darracq	Long Island
1908	G. Robertson	Locomobile	Long Island
1909	H. Grant	Alco	Long Island
1910	H. Grant	Alco	Long Island
1911	R. Mulford	Lozier	Savannah
1912	R. de Palma	Mercedes	Milwaukee
1914	R. de Palma	Mercedes	Santa Monica
1915	D. Resta	Peugeot	San Francisco
1916	D. Resta	Peugeot	Santa Monica

33

Chapter 6

The First Grand Prix

France 1906

It was the French who finally changed the face of motor sport. Although they had been capturing their share of victories in the marathon races of the first three or four years of the twentieth century, they had begun to resent the regulations which limited each competing country to three cars. 'Why should we, the cradle of the sport, and with more motor manufacturers than any other country, be allowed only three miserable entries just as some little one-car nations?' they grumbled, and proceeded to set up another race to their own regulations at Le Mans.

So the Gordon Bennett races died and the new 103 kilometre circuit at Le Mans became the mecca of the motor sporting fraternity. Now each *manufacturer* was allowed to enter three cars, a much more palatable arrangement for French interests. The race was to be run in two six-lap daily sections. Parts of the big three-sided circuit were in good repair—a bit bumpy and dusty (or bumpy and muddy, dependent on weather) but that was normal. However the link road joining the two main arms of the triangle (built to avoid racing through the narrow roads of the village of St. Calais), was rough and in parts made up of temporary planks.

This first Grand Prix de l'Automobile Club de France (although at the time it was called the ninth after the capital-to-capital races and others) was run

The 65-mile circuit used for the first Grand Prix was tarred to lay the dust. It succeeded—but the melting tar proved as hazardous as swirling dust.

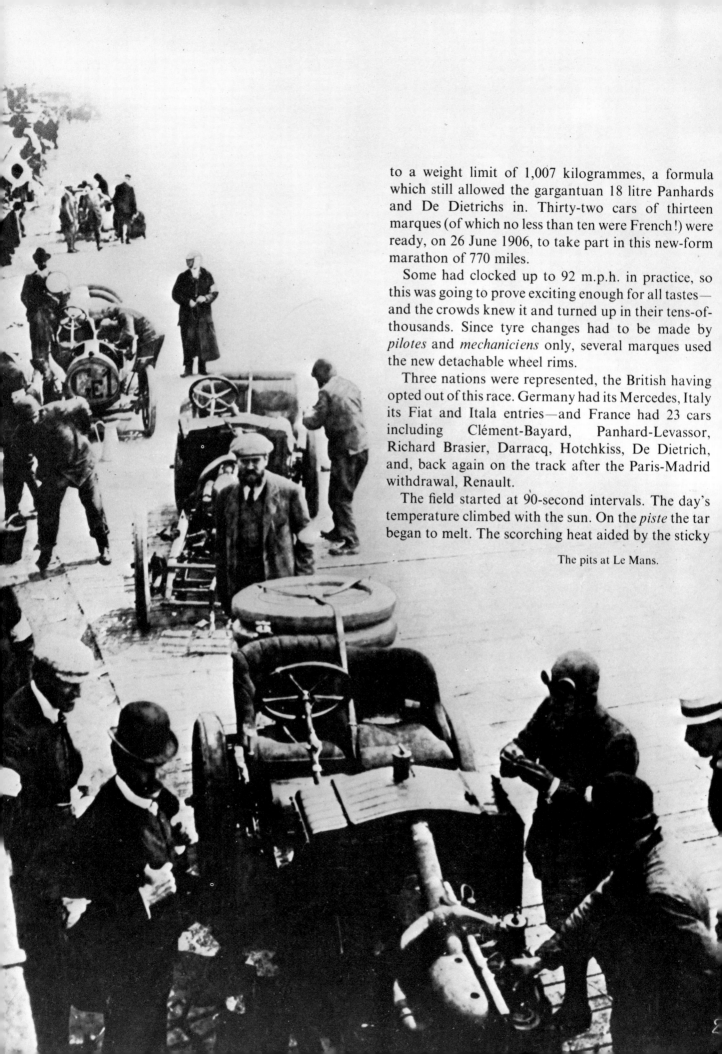

to a weight limit of 1,007 kilogrammes, a formula which still allowed the gargantuan 18 litre Panhards and De Dietrichs in. Thirty-two cars of thirteen marques (of which no less than ten were French!) were ready, on 26 June 1906, to take part in this new-form marathon of 770 miles.

Some had clocked up to 92 m.p.h. in practice, so this was going to prove exciting enough for all tastes— and the crowds knew it and turned up in their tens-of-thousands. Since tyre changes had to be made by *pilotes* and *mechaniciens* only, several marques used the new detachable wheel rims.

Three nations were represented, the British having opted out of this race. Germany had its Mercedes, Italy its Fiat and Itala entries—and France had 23 cars including Clément-Bayard, Panhard-Levassor, Richard Brasier, Darracq, Hotchkiss, De Dietrich, and, back again on the track after the Paris-Madrid withdrawal, Renault.

The field started at 90-second intervals. The day's temperature climbed with the sun. On the *piste* the tar began to melt. The scorching heat aided by the sticky

The pits at Le Mans.

tar surface began to damage tyres, and some crews had to change the entire set at least ten times—no joke in an era when one slashed off the ruined rubber with knives and fingernails, bolted the new ones on, pumped up again by hand, then swung the starting handle of an engine as capacious as a modern truck.

Almost as soon as battle commenced reports of casualties began to come in. A Hotchkiss driver ran off the course, chewing up his wheel spokes. Calling on his team-mates for help, he cannibalized a few from each of their cars, spent an hour or two cutting and fitting—and continued on his way. Several others had to give up the race when they were temporarily blinded by liquid tar, and one driver gave up the ghost from sheer exhaustion in the first day's hammering heat.

The first lap went to three Brasiers, and the second lap saw them all out of the race with breakdowns. On the third lap the 90 h.p. 13 litre Renault conducted by Hungarian Ferenc Szisz took the lead, chased by three Fiats and the rest of the pack. He held this lead for the first day and recorded a respectable average of 65 m.p.h. on the hot fast circuit.

The second day, and Szisz again took the lead, hounded by Felice Nazarro in his Fiat. Both halted several times for the usual punctures, and in a race of over 12 hours, the astonishing fact is that the victorious Renault beat the Fiat by less than a minute.

Those two days in June long ago established the present Grand Prix series with its world championship of drivers, and also established the agricultural district of

Above
A 'streamlined' Renault, piloted by French driver Edmond during the previous year's Gordon Bennett eliminating trials at Clermont-Ferrand—the last of the series that led to the Grands Prix.

Right
Thirty-two cars of 13 different marques were entered in the 1906 Grand Prix. This is the 100 h.p. 1906 Mercedes.

the Sarthe, and Le Mans in particular, as the home of
one of the world's best-known motor races.

The following year the French Grand Prix was won
in reverse order—by Nazarro with Szisz in second
place—the third of three great Fiat victories in 1907.
The first had been won on the incredibly dangerous
roads of Sicily in the new race organized by wealthy
Vincenzo Florio for the first time in 1906. Fiat gained a
second success in the Kaiserpreis Race, the event in
which the German Emperor had offered his special
cup and prize. Nazarro won the heat and the final of
this race, held in the Taunus Mountains near Frank-
furt, with colleagues Wagner and Lancia in fifth
and sixth places.

Meanwhile, in England, on the Brooklands estate
in Surrey, the first real motor racing track was staging
its inaugural races. In a country where the 20 m.p.h.
speed limit still held back progress, this was indeed a
bold move, and the races there helped spur the awaken-
ing British motor industry—although the local in-
habitants (this was the stockbroker belt of Surrey)
made loud noises of protest. Racing and record-
breaking nevertheless continued at Brooklands with a
short break during World War I, until 1939 when it
was used for wartime purposes and thus became lost to
motor sport for ever.

Chapter 7

The Fast Ones

Land Speed Records

A Frenchman, the Comte Gaston de Chasseloup-Laubat, began it all. In December 1898 he drove his Jeantaud electric car to a stretch of road at Achères, near Paris, and was there timed to cover a measured kilometre at 39.24 m.p.h. He was, he proclaimed, the fastest man on earth.

A Belgian named Camille Jenatzy, known because of his red hair and beard as the 'Red Devil', accepted the challenge inherent in Chasseloup-Laubat's announcement. He had built an electric car of his own design. It was cigar-shaped on its bogey, had tiller steering, and was named by its creator, *La Jamais Contente*. Jenatzy drove it to the same stretch of road and was timed at 41.42 m.p.h. The first duel for the world land speed record had begun.

Chasseloup-Laubat returned and reached 43.69 m.p.h. Jenatzy replied with 49.92 m.p.h. Chasseloup-Laubat got up to 57.60 m.p.h. and Jenatzy retorted with 65.79 m.p.h. And it all happened within a space of five months.

There the duel ended, with Jenatzy's the fastest speed record ever to be credited to an electric car. The two had reached the limits of their cars' electrical systems and the general public were relieved, for it was a widely held belief that a man would not be able to breathe at a speed of over 70 m.p.h.

Camille Jenatzy's *Jamais Contente* sets the world land speed record in 1899.

Right
The 1909 Blitzenbenz *Weltrekordwagen.* This 200 h.p. car clocked 125.95 m.p.h. at Brooklands with Hémery at the wheel.

That misapprehension was to be shattered within three years when a streamlined steam car built and driven by Léon Serpollet reached 75.06 m.p.h. along the palm-fringed Promenade des Anglais at Nice.

Henry Ford—World Record Holder
An American and a petrol-engined car took over when W. K. Vanderbilt raised the record to 76.08 m.p.h. at Ablis, near Chartres in a Paris-Vienna Mors in 1902. Henry Fournier capped this in a similar car with 76.60 m.p.h. later in the year, his being the first record to be set with mechanical timing instead of hand-held watches.

The following year saw the entry to the speed lists of the remarkable Gobron-Brillié—the product of a Paris factory. Its chisel-shaped bow contained a four-foot long, 4 cylinder engine of 15 litres capacity with double pistons. Arthur Duray drove it at 84.73 m.p.h.

The 90 m.p.h. mark was passed for the first time in America by car-maker Henry Ford driving *999*: a red 4 cylinder car with no gears, clutch or body. It was no more than a flat bed with a seat, a 'special' which was the forerunner of many record contenders.

Ford took the car to Anchor Bay, north east of Detroit, while it was frozen over. A team of farmers scraped snow from the ice and scattered cinders to give the car's wheels some grip, and Ford reached 91.37 m.p.h., though his record was not recognized in Europe because of the lack of status of the American club that provided the timekeepers.

Above left
Unofficial record from the United States. This spidery Oldsmobile covered a mile in 42 seconds in 1903 at Daytona Beach.

Left
Henry Ford's famous 999 with Barney Oldfield at the wheel. The race-and-record car brought Ford a brief land speed title in 1904.

Vanderbilt, who took a 90 Mercedes across Daytona Beach, Florida, a fortnight later and reached 92.30 m.p.h. was also denied world recognition. But a few weeks later L. E. Rigolly achieved 94.78 m.p.h. at Nice in the Gobron-Brillié, and shortly afterwards Baron Pierre de Caters, a Belgian, drove a Mercedes along Ostend promenade at 97.26 m.p.h.

The 'Ton'
Only a few years had passed since 70 m.p.h. had been scoffed at by some as an impossible speed. Now the question had become, who would be first to beat the magic 'ton'?

It was, in fact, Rigolly again in the Gobron-Brillié. He reached 103.56 m.p.h. at Ostend, and it is worth bearing in mind that even today, just on seven decades later, the majority of motorists have never driven at over 100 m.p.h.

Up to this time Britain had not been in a position to challenge the record because of the absence of long, straight, unrestricted roads, but in 1905 S. F. Edge's 6 cylinder 90 h.p. Napier was sent out to Daytona

Right
American Bob Burman scored a land speed record after beating Oldfield's 1910 speed by 2.3 m.p.h., and again in 1911, in the Benz, making it three in a row for the German company. He is seen here with the car at a race.

and, although the sand was bumpy, Arthur Macdonald took it to 104.65 m.p.h.

Steam made a brief return to the lists in 1906 when Fred Marriott drove a Stanley at 121.57 m.p.h. at Daytona, but this was steam's last record.

Three years later came the first record to be set in Britain, when Victor Hémery in a four-cylinder Blitzen Benz clocked 125.95 m.p.h. on the Brooklands racing circuit, which had been opened two years earlier. In America the colourful Barney Oldfield clamped a cigar stub between his teeth and reached 131.72 m.p.h. in a Benz but this, too, was denied recognition as a world record.

Up to this time speeds had been accepted as records on a one-way run basis. But now, to discount the advantage to be gained from a tail wind, it was ruled that speeds must be the average of two runs in opposite directions. As a result speeds dropped for a time.

The last record to be set up before the outbreak of World War I was at Brooklands in 1914 when L. G.

'Cupid' Hornsted drove a 4 cylinder 21½ litre Benz at 124.1 m.p.h. His record was to stand until 1922 when Kenelm Lee Guinness reached 133.75 m.p.h. at Brooklands in a 350 h.p. aircraft-engined Sunbeam.

This was the last time the record was to be broken on a racing circuit. And two years later the record was broken for the last time on an ordinary road—by Ernest Eldridge in a 300 h.p. Fiat. Carrying a passenger, he achieved 145.90 m.p.h. near Paris.

The Campbell-Segrave Era
Record-breaking entered then on its most glamorous era, with rich sportsmen spending fortunes on developing the most potent specialized machinery and travelling the world in the quest to be the fastest men alive.

The first of these new heroes was Captain (later Sir) Malcolm Campbell, who had taken over the Guinness Sunbeam. He had it fitted with a new body and a longer tail and named it *Bluebird*. His first attempts on the record were unfortunate. Several times he beat it but

was robbed of glory by timekeeping failures. On Fanoe
Island, Denmark, he was doing 140 m.p.h. when the
tyres left his rear wheels. On a later run he lost a front
tyre, went into the spectators and killed a boy.

Back in Britain in 1924 he went to Pendine sands in
Wales, hit 146.16 m.p.h. and the record was his. Next
year he improved it to 150.87 m.p.h. But in 1926
Major (later Sir) Henry Segrave went to Southport
sands in the north of England and in a Coatalen-
designed Sunbeam with a 4 litre V12 engine reached
152.33 m.p.h. And then Parry Thomas, a Welsh
engineer known as the 'Flying Celt', went to Pendine
with a 12 cylinder 27 litre 400 h.p. Liberty aero engine
in a car called *Babs* and averaged 171.09 m.p.h.

Campbell went back to Pendine and, after the
beach had been cleared of stones, reached 174.88
m.p.h. Thomas returned to Pendine in pursuit,

crashed at nearly 170 m.p.h. and was killed. His car was buried in the sand, to be exhumed a few years ago.

Segrave heard the news on board a ship to America and Daytona. He carried on, lost his brakes on his first run and had to drive into the sea to stop. But before he left he had averaged 203.79 m.p.h.—faster than many aircraft of the time. Campbell followed him to Daytona and reached 206.96 m.p.h.

Understandably, Americans were piqued. Frank Lockhart's bid to take the record with a 16 cylinder Stutz cost him his life, but Ray Keech in his Triplex, with three Liberty engines (one in front of him and two behind) totalling 81 litres, clocked 207.5 m.p.h.

Back came Segrave in 1928 in a new *Golden Arrow* with aiming sights on the bonnet. He reached 231.44 m.p.h. and received a knighthood in a blaze of patriotic acclaim.

Enter Eyston and Cobb

It was Segrave's last land speed record. In the first half of the thirties Campbell returned again and again to America, improving his record until at Bonneville, Utah, in 1935 he passed 300 m.p.h.

Bonneville was to be the scene of most attempts from this point on. Captain George Eyston went there with *Thunderbolt*, a seven-ton, 73 litre twin Rolls-Royce engined car, took the record, and found himself in a duel with John Cobb, a big, shy, fur broker, born in 1899, the year Jenatzy beat a mile a minute.

With his four-wheel drive Railton, Cobb passed 350 m.p.h. for the first time as the war clouds loomed in 1938. The last record before the war also went to Cobb at 369.70 m.p.h. At Bonneville in 1947 Cobb came back to clock 394.20 m.p.h.—and that record lasted through until 1964. Interest in the land speed

Bluebird-Proteus; 403.10 m.p.h. at Lake Eyre, Australia in July 1964. This car was the rebuilt Bluebird I, which crashed during a record attempt at Utah in 1960.

In 1965 Robert Summers of America in *Goldenrod*, powered by four petrol-injection Chrysler engines totalling 27,924 c.c. and developing about 2,400 b.h.p. took the wheel-driven land speed record up as far as 409.27 m.p.h.

But by this time a jet car had passed 500 m.p.h. There was still a compulsion to be the fastest man on wheels. But it was no longer possible to be fastest in a wheel-driven piston-engined car. This could no longer have more than the status of a class record, for it had ceased to represent the ultimate achievement. A chapter of history had ended.

Some key dates and names in the establishment of land speed records by wheel-driven cars

Year	Driver (Car)	Speed
1898	G. de Chasseloup-Laubat (Jeantaux electric)	39.24 m.p.h.
1899	C. Jenatzy (Jenatzy electric)	65.79 m.p.h.
1902	L. Serpollet (Serpollet steamer)	75.06 m.p.h.
1902	M. Augières (Mors)	77.13 m.p.h.
1903	A. Duray (Gobron-Brillié)	84.73 m.p.h.
1904	L. Rigolly (Gobron-Brillié)	103.55 m.p.h.
1904	P. Baras (Darracq)	104.52 m.p.h.
1905	V. Hémery (Darracq)	109.65 m.p.h.
1906	F. Marriott (Stanley steamer)	121.57 m.p.h.
1909	V. Hémery (Benz)	125.95 m.p.h.
1910	B. Oldfield (Benz)	131.72 m.p.h.
1922	K. Guinness (Sunbeam)	133.75 m.p.h.
1924	M. Campbell (Sunbeam)	146.16 m.p.h.
1925	M. Campbell (Sunbeam)	150.87 m.p.h.
1926	P. Thomas (Thomas Special)	171.02 m.p.h.
1927	H. Segrave (Sunbeam)	203.79 m.p.h.
1928	R. Keech (White Triplex)	207.55 m.p.h.
1929	H. Segrave (Irving-Napier)	231.44 m.p.h.
1932	M. Campbell (Napier-Campbell)	253.97 m.p.h.
1933	M. Campbell (Campbell Special)	272.46 m.p.h.
1935	M. Campbell (Campbell Special)	301.13 m.p.h.
1937	G. Eyston (Thunderbolt)	312.00 m.p.h.
1938	G. Eyston (Thunderbolt)	357.50 m.p.h.
1939	J. Cobb (Railton)	369.70 m.p.h.
1947	J. Cobb (Railton)	394.20 m.p.h.
1964	D. Campbell (Bluebird-Proteus)	403.10 m.p.h.
1965	R. Summers (Goldenrod)	409.27 m.p.h.

record, so specialized, so far removed from everyday motoring, had waned.

But another Campbell had two reasons for wanting the record. Donald was the son of Sir Malcolm and he had an obsession to prove himself as bold and skilful as his father. He was also an old-fashioned patriot, with a blazing desire to see Britain hold every record in existence. He named his £1 million turbo-jet-engined car *Bluebird* after his father's cars, and in 1964 on dried-up Lake Eyre in Australia, he eventually took it to 403.10 m.p.h.

Few people cared greatly. Already Craig Breedlove of America had gone faster in a much cheaper three-wheeled car propelled by jet thrust. Campbell's was to be almost the last record bid in a wheel-driven car. He died in 1967 and curiously, like Segrave and Cobb, he died chasing the world water speed record.

Chapter 8

Endurance Races

The Big Three

When it became clear that the town-to-town races were at an end and that some doubts existed about the development of the circuit races, a number of people who felt that real motor racing was a question of endurance more than anything else, set about finding a way to keep their ideas alive—ideas which would fit in with the official thinking of the time.

No one can be said to have done more in this direction than Vincenzo Florio, a wealthy Sicilian who had long had a passion for motor cars. It is said that at one time he employed the great Felice Nazzaro as a sort of superior chauffeur (Nazzaro had appeared on the Florio estate with a few Fiats bought by Vincenzo) and it is even claimed that it was during the four years that he was with Florio that Nazzaro received his basic training as a racing driver.

Land-owner Florio had made a practice of organizing private races in the grounds of his house, with friends and chauffeur as principal competitors, and out of these domestic events grew Florio's ambition to launch a big 'official' motor race in Sicily. The main difficulty was that there were practically no roads on the island—and worse, robber bands lived in the mountains. However, after attending the last of the Gordon Bennett races in 1905 Florio, in conversation with Henri Desgrange, the Editor of *L'Auto* formu-

A typical Targa Florio scene; three generations of Sicilians have watched this classic race.

Above
Felice Nazzaro acknowledges
the cheers of the crowd and the
officials as he passes the line,
winner of the 1907 Targa
Florio.

Below
Targa country, pioneer
days. Here Vincenzo Lancia
drives through a village in his
28/40 h.p. Fiat.

lated the idea of a race in Sicily—and the following year the Targa Florio was announced. A Parisian goldsmith was commissioned to make a gold plate—the Targa—as a trophy.

The first race was held on Sunday, 6 May 1906, and although there should have been 22 entrants only 10 starters actually turned up due to a variety of difficulties—not the least of which was the fear that the mountain bandits would probably use them as moving snap-shooting targets.

The roads were appalling and the problems considerable; but Florio pressed on, and over the years with many changes of circuits—longer ones, shorter ones, some reaching very great altitudes, and others staying nearer sea level—the race went on. From 1919 to 1930 a circuit of only 108 km, called the 'Medium Madonie', was adopted and it was on this circuit that European racing was revived after World War I—incidentally on that occasion the first driver to set off was none other than Enzo Ferrari, of later fame.

The Targa Florio, the oldest and most romantic of the endurance races, has had its ups and downs and its moments of greatness, but it has remained steadfastly in the sporting calendar, and although the cars which now compete must be very far removed from the kind of vehicle that Vincenzo Florio first envisaged, it is the last of the genuine road races.

Above
The nineteenth Targa, 1928. A quick wheel change for the 1500 Alfa Romeo.

Below
In 1924 and 1925 the Coppa Florio, an older race inaugurated by Vincenzo Florio, was run concurrently with the Targa. Here a Peugeot competes in the 1925 event.

Targa Florio Winners

Date	Circuit	Winner
1906	Big Madonie	Cagno (Itala) 29.1 m.p.h.
1907	Big Madonie	Nazarro (Fiat) 33.6 m.p.h.
1908	Big Madonie	Trucco (Isotta Fraschini) 37.2 m.p.h.
1909	Big Madonie	Cluppa (Spa) 34.0 m.p.h.
1910	Big Madonie	Cariolato (France) 29.2 m.p.h.
1911	Big Madonie	Ceirano (Scat) 29.1 m.p.h.
1912	Round Sicily	Snipe (Scat) 26.5 m.p.h.
1913	Round Sicily	Nazzaro (Nazzaro) 33.8 m.p.h.
1914	Round Sicily	Ceirano (Scat) 38.7 m.p.h.
1919	Medium Madonie	André Boillot (Peugeot) 34.2 m.p.h.
1920	Medium Madonie	Meregalli (Nazzaro) 36.0 m.p.h.
1921	Medium Madonie	Masetti (Fiat) 36.2 m.p.h.
1922	Medium Madonie	Masetti (Mercedes) 39.2 m.p.h.
1923	Medium Madonie	Sivocci (Alfa Romeo) 36.7 m.p.h.
1924	Medium Madonie	Werner (Mercedes) 41.0 m.p.h.
1925	Medium Madonie	Costantini (Bugatti) 44.5 m.p.h.
1926	Medium Madonie	Costantini (Bugatti) 45.7 m.p.h.
1927	Medium Madonie	Materassi (Bugatti) 44.2 m.p.h.
1928	Medium Madonie	Divo (Bugatti) 45.6 m.p.h.
1929	Medium Madonie	Divo (Bugatti) 46.2 m.p.h.
1930	Medium Madonie	Varzi (Alfa Romeo) 48.5 m.p.h.
1931	Big Madonie	Nuvolari (Alfa Romeo) 40.3 m.p.h.
1932	Little Madonie	Nuvolari (Alfa Romeo) 49.3 m.p.h.
1933	Little Madonie	Brivio (Alfa Romeo) 47.5 m.p.h.
1934	Little Madonie	Varzi (Alfa Romeo) 43.0 m.p.h.
1935	Little Madonie	Brivio (Alfa Romeo) 49.2 m.p.h.
1936	Little Madonie	Magistri (Lancia) 41.7 m.p.h.
1937	Favorita Park	Severi (Maserati) 66.9 m.p.h.
1938	Favorita Park	Rocco (Maserati) 71.0 m.p.h.

Above
Officials make a dash for it as a Mille Miglia car gets away fast from a control point. This picture was taken from another competing car.

Right
Mille Miglia 1957. Mechanics tend to Peter Collins' Ferrari at a pit stop.

Left
Le Mans 1972.

Date	Circuit	Winner	Date	Circuit	Winner
1939	Favorita Park	Villoresi (Maserati) 84.8 m.p.h.	1960	Little Madonie	Bonnier and Herrmann (Porsche) 59.20 m.p.h.
1940	Favorita Park	Villoresi (Maserati) 88.4 m.p.h.	1961	Little Madonie	von Trips and Gendebien (Ferrari) 64.3 m.p.h.
1948	Round Sicily	Biondetti and Igor (Ferrari) 55.1 m.p.h.	1962	Little Madonie	Rodriguez, Mairesse and Gendebien (Ferrari) 63.4 m.p.h.
1949	Round Sicily	Biondetti and Benedetti (Ferrari) 50.6 m.p.h.	1963	Little Madonie	Bonnier and Abate (Porsche) 64.5 m.p.h.
1950	Round Sicily	Bornigia and Bornigia (Alfa Romeo) 54.0 m.p.h.	1964	Little Madonie	Davis and Pucci (Porsche) 62.3 m.p.h.
1951	Little Madonie	Cortese (Frazer-Nash) 47.6 m.p.h.	1965	Little Madonie	Bandini and Vaccarella (Ferrari) 63.7 m.p.h.
1952	Little Madonie	Bonetto (Lancia) 49.7 m.p.h.	1966	Little Madonie	Mairesse and Muller (Porsche) 61.5 m.p.h.
1953	Little Madonie	Maglioli (Lancia) 50.1 m.p.h.	1967	Little Madonie	Hawkins and Stommelen (Porsche) 67.6 m.p.h.
1954	Little Madonie	Taruffi (Lancia) 55.9 m.p.h.	1968	Little Madonie	Elford and Maglioli (Porsche) 69.0 m.p.h.
1955	Little Madonie	Moss and Collins (Mercedes-Benz) 59.80 m.p.h.	1969	Little Madonie	Mitter and Schutz (Porsche) 73.0 m.p.h.
1956	Little Madonie	Maglioli (Porsche) 56.5 m.p.h.	1970	Little Madonie	Siffert and Redman (Porsche) 74.7 m.p.h.
1958	Little Madonie	Musso and Gendebien (Ferrari) 58.9 m.p.h.	1971	Little Madonie	Vaccarella and Hezemans (Alfa Romeo) 74.6 m.p.h.
1959	Little Madonie	Barth and Seidel (Porsche) 56.7 m.p.h.	1972	Little Madonie	Merzario and Munari (Ferrari) 76.14 m.p.h.

Endurance at Le Mans

It was not until the clouds of World War I had blown away that another race, similar in some ways to the Targa Florio, yet with a different basic purpose, was born. There had been considerable interest in motor sport in the town of Le Mans—the first Grand Prix had been fought there in 1906, and other races had followed. In 1920 an international voiturette race had been held there and repeated the next two years on the new *Circuit Permanent de la Sarthe*, and French enthusiasts began to plan a regular annual event. Two people were in the centre of the discussion, journalist Charles Faroux, and Georges Durant, engineer and racing enthusiast; their talks resulted in a new form of racing—a round-the-clock contest.

This was to be a race of men and vehicles with whom the ordinary public could readily identify, for already Grand Prix was becoming so esoteric that the motor racing fan without a highly specialized knowledge of the high-speed machinery was beginning to lose the thread of the technical advances developed by racing, and spectator-enthusiasm was waning.

From the very start the founders laid down three conditions. Firstly that entry should be limited to cars performing strictly to the description in the ordinary catalogue published that year by the manufacturer. Secondly that competing cars had to carry touring bodywork, to be equipped with wings, running boards, headlamps, tail and side lamps, hood, horns, rear-view mirror, and lastly (except those under 1100 c.c.) all cars should carry four-seater bodywork.

It was out of these very simple beginnings that the great 24 hours race of Le Mans began. In early years there were numbers of interesting and ingenious regulations—one of which required cars to perform a number of laps with their hoods up—and a very strict control of this regulation was always exercised. Many a time valuable minutes were lost as an unfortunate competitor tangled with a complex canvas-and-metal hood to the delight of rivals and the distress of his pit staff.

Over the years the circuit was modified so that it no longer ran into the environs of Le Mans, and became the kind of circuit it now is—8.36 miles long. (Towards

Above
Le Mans 1928—Bentley wins again, with Barnato and Rubin driving.

Below
The gendarmes have seen it all before . . . Paddy Hopkirk in an MGB in the Esses, 1964.

Right
Hats off to Aston Martin, Le Mans winner 1959 with Roy Salvadori and Carroll Shelby sharing the wheel.

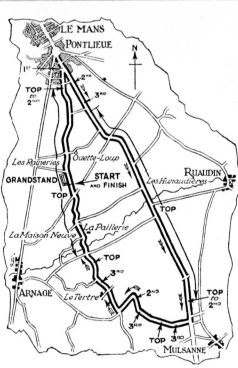

Above
Le Mans circuit 1920; the basis of today's *Circuit Permanent de la Sarthe*. The Pontlieu section was cut off in 1929 and later the circuit acquired the Esses and Tertre Rouge.

Left
Into the Esses (S-bends) in the
'60s. An MG tails an Alfa
Romeo into the first bend . . .

Right
. . . and the Esses in the '70s—a
clutch of cars swing through
the second section, a right-
hander.

the end of the 'twenties came the great Bentley victories (four years in succession) which gave Great Britain absolute precedence in the world of sports cars. After the collapse of Bentley Motors, the Italians and French found time to make Le Mans their own, and it was not until after the war when the Jaguar assault was launched that Britain was once again able to re-assert its position in the race.)

It was about this time that the Americans first became seriously interested in the event, and in 1950 Briggs Cunningham first entered two Cadillac cars, one a perfectly ordinary saloon, the other a curiously square and slab-sided open car—which was incidentally the least successful of the two. Cunningham went on to produce cars of his own design and manufacture powered by other American engines, but was never able to achieve complete success.

Towards the end of the 'fifties the honours were divided between Jaguar (1951, 1953, 1955, 1956, 1957),

Ferrari (1954, 1958) and Aston Martin (1959). From 1960 Ferrari won for six consecutive years. Throughout this latter period the Ford Motor Company had done everything in its power to wrest victory from the Italians. Ford had spent an enormous amount of money developing the GT40 which made its debut in 1964, and each year saw a fresh battle between these two companies. Finally in 1966 Ford achieved a victory which they repeated in 1967, 1968 and 1969. However, by that time the regulations had moved so far from the original conception that the scene became somewhat confused. The admission of prototypes has no doubt in some respects increased the interest in the race, but the truth is that Le Mans today is not what its originators intended it to be, and it remains to be seen whether it will continue as one of the great endurance races, or indeed whether it will fade from interest. Perhaps an answer would be to return to the original regulations.

Le Mans Winners

Date	Winner	
1923	Lagache and Leonard (Chenard-Walcker)	57.2 m.p.h.
1924	Duff and Clement (Bentley)	53.7 m.p.h.
1925	de Courcelles and Rossignol (La Lorraine)	57.8 m.p.h.
1926	Bloch and Rossignol (La Lorraine)	66.0 m.p.h.
1927	Benjafield and Davis (Bentley)	61.3 m.p.h.
1928	Barnato and Rubin (Bentley)	69.1 m.p.h.
1929	Barnato and Birkin (Bentley)	73.6 m.p.h.
1930	Barnato and Kidston (Bentley)	75.8 m.p.h.
1931	Lord Howe and Birkin (Alfa Romeo)	78.1 m.p.h.
1932	Sommer and Chinetti (Alfa Romeo)	76.4 m.p.h.
1933	Sommer and Nuvolari (Alfa Romeo)	81.4 m.p.h.
1934	Chinetti and Etancelin (Alfa Romeo)	74.7 m.p.h.
1935	Hindmarsh and Fontes (Lagonda)	77.8 m.p.h.
1937	Wimille and Benoist (Bugatti)	85.1 m.p.h.
1938	Chaboud and Tremoulet (Delahaye)	82.3 m.p.h.
1939	Wimille and Veyron (Bugatti)	86.8 m.p.h.
1949	Lord Selsdon and Chinetti (Ferrari)	82.2 m.p.h.

Date	Winner	
1950	Rosier (father and son) (Talbot)	89.7 m.p.h.
1951	Walker and Whitehead (Jaguar)	93.5 m.p.h.
1952	Lang and Riess (Mercedes-Benz)	96.6 m.p.h.
1953	Rolt and Hamilton (Jaguar)	105.8 m.p.h.
1954	Gonzales and Trintignant (Ferrari)	105.1 m.p.h.
1955	Hawthorn and Bueb (Jaguar)	107.0 m.p.h.
1956	Flockhart and Sanderson (Jaguar)	104.4 m.p.h.
1957	Flockhart and Bueb (Jaguar)	113.8 m.p.h.
1958	P. Hill and Gendebien (Ferrari)	106.2 m.p.h.
1959	Salvadori and Shelby (Aston Martin)	112.5 m.p.h.
1960	Frère and Gendebien (Ferrari)	109.2 m.p.h.
1961	P. Hill and Gendebien (Ferrari)	115.9 m.p.h.
1962	P. Hill and Gendebien (Ferrari)	115.2 m.p.h.
1963	Scarfiotti and Bandini (Ferrari)	118.1 m.p.h.
1964	Guichet and Vaccarella (Ferrari)	121.5 m.p.h.
1965	Rindt and Gregory (Ferrari)	121.1 m.p.h.
1966	McLaren and Amon (Ford)	125.4 m.p.h.
1967	Gurney and Foyt (Ford)	135.4 m.p.h.
1968	P. Rodriguez and Bianchi (Ford)	115.3 m.p.h.
1969	Ickx and Oliver (Ford)	129.4 m.p.h.
1970	Attwood and Herrmann (Porsche)	119.3 m.p.h.
1971	van Lennep and Marko (Porsche)	138.1 m.p.h.
1972	Pescarolo and Hill (Matra-Simca)	121.4 m.p.h.

Classic Italian

First run just four years later than Le Mans was another colourful race of almost equal importance in the field of endurance—the Mille Miglia. Although again different in conception there is no doubt that this event was inspired by the success of the Targa Florio and the Le Mans 24 hours. This public-road marathon was born of the enthusiasm of three men— Count Maggi, Franco Mazzotti and Giovanni Canestrini—who planned a long, tough race which would run over the northern half of the Italian peninsular, from Brescia in the north to Rome in the south. It was to cover a 1,000 miles (the old Roman mile of a thousand paces) and to be called the *Mille Miglia*.

The cars were started at one-minute intervals, and travelled over open roads in much the way as the original great inter-city races. The original course, a great figure-of-eight occupying the middle of the Italian peninsular, although changed in detail from

Below
A thousand miles of Italian roads—the Mille Miglia route.

Below right
Moss brings the 300 SLR back to Brescia at a winning average of 97.897 m.p.h.

Mille Miglia Winners

Date	Winner	
1927	Minoia and Morandi (OM)	48.0 m.p.h.
1928	Campari and Ramponi (Alfa Romeo)	52.3 m.p.h.
1929	Campari and Ramponi (Alfa Romeo)	55.7 m.p.h.
1930	Nuvolari and Guidotti (Alfa Romeo)	62.4 m.p.h.
1931	Caracciola and Sebastian (Mercedes)	62.9 m.p.h.
1932	Borzacchini and Bignami (Alfa Romeo)	68.3 m.p.h.
1933	Nuvolari and Compagnoni (Alfa Romeo)	67.5 m.p.h.
1934	Varzi and Bignami (Alfa Romeo)	71.0 m.p.h.
1935	Pintacuda and Della Stufa (Alfa Romeo)	71.3 m.p.h.
1936	Brivio and Ongaro (Alfa Romeo)	75.6 m.p.h.
1937	Pintacuda and Mambelli (Alfa Romeo)	71.3 m.p.h.
1938	Biondetti and Stefani (Alfa Romeo)	84.1 m.p.h.
1940	Hanstein and Baumer (BMW)	103.6 m.p.h.
1947	Biondetti and Romano (Alfa Romeo)	69.7 m.p.h.
1948	Biondetti and Navona (Ferrari)	75.3 m.p.h.
1949	Biondetti and Salani (Ferrari)	81.7 m.p.h.
1950	Marzotto and Crosara (Ferrari)	76.6 m.p.h.
1951	Villoresi and Cassani (Ferrari)	75.7 m.p.h.
1952	Bracco and Rolfo (Ferrari)	79.9 m.p.h.
1953	Marzotto and Crosara (Ferrari)	88.5 m.p.h.
1954	Ascari (Lancia)	86.8 m.p.h.
1955	Moss and Jenkinson (Mercedes)	97.9 m.p.h.
1956	Castellotti (Ferrari)	85.4 m.p.h.
1957	Taruffi (Ferrari)	94.8 m.p.h.

time to time, remained throughout the life of the race consistent in its basic route and character. Local knowledge always proved to be a vital factor in the event, and it was usually an Italian 'benefit' for both cars and driver, save for a couple of onslaughts by Mercedes Benz, once in the period between the wars, and in 1955, the year of one of the greatest victories, when Stirling Moss with his passenger Denis Jenkinson broke all the records and most of the legends associated with the race.

An unhappy accident in 1938 nearly brought the race to an end when a number of people were killed and Government opposition was so great that it was not held at all in 1939. The race was revived in 1947 and continued until once more an accident, this time of even greater proportions (the Marquis de Portago with an American passenger Edward Nelson crashed into the crowd of spectators, killing themselves and eleven others) ended for ever the Mille Miglia in its original form. Some will say that such an unhappy event was predictable, for the same dangers were present as in the early inter-capital battles, but the fact remains that in the Mille Miglia, more than in any other event, the great endurance races dating from the dawn of the motor era were kept alive; and it is true to say, whatever the excitements of other forms of racing there remains, in the great surviving endurance events, a special kind of magic without which motor sport would not be quite the same.

Racing Vintage

Below
Vintage greyhound. A 1934 Derby-Maserati.

Right
Bentleys, MGs, Austin Sevens, and a dozen other marques crowd into the paddock at a Vintage meeting before the start of a handicap race.

Right
Two 1925 1½ litre Frazer Nash cars battle it out at Lodge Corner, Oulton Park.

Far right
Mrs. Arnold-Foster takes her spindly 1921 GN round the circuit at Cheshire's Oulton Park on a vintage gala day.

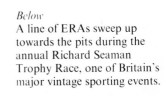

Below
A line of ERAs sweep up
towards the pits during the
annual Richard Seaman
Trophy Race, one of Britain's
major vintage sporting events.

Chapter 9

Indianapolis

The Powerhouse

'Suppose we allowed four-wheel drive? In two years' time, nothing would have changed—except that we should all have spent $10,000 more on our cars.' Thus spoke Bobby Unser, winning driver in the 1968 race at the Indianapolis Motor Speedway, in defence of the United States Auto Club ruling that after 1969 four-wheel drive entries would be excluded.

Unser had grasped the essential fact that speedway racing is entertainment, although when, back in 1908, Carl Fisher envisaged the closed circuit at Indianapolis, he expected that it would be used by the Indiana vehicle builders for testing purposes as well as for competition. In those days, the mere ability to keep moving was a selling point for a vehicle, and the circuit was laid out for endurance runs, in a rectangle with straights of five furlongs and one furlong and slightly-banked constant-radius turns each a quarter of a mile long.

But at that same time Henry Ford had mastered the problems of mere mobility with his model T, with its detachable cylinder head, high-tension ignition with low-tension distributor, epicyclic gearbox and enclosed drive line. The time had come to devote engineering effort to cutting the cost of production; Ford and his copyists leaped ahead, and the Detroit area became the centre of the automotive industry.

The year is 1965; Jim Clark wins at Indianapolis. Here seen leading a pack that includes A. J. Foyt, Dan Gurney and Parnelli Jones, Clark won the Indianapolis 500 at an average speed of 150.69 m.p.h. in his Lotus-Ford.

But while the demand for a test track in Indiana faded away, the circuit flourished on spectator sports.

Indianapolis Balloon Race

The very first event was a balloon race in June, 1909. The track was opened in August, but the surface of crushed stone and asphalt broke up rapidly, causing fatal accidents. The best paving material then known was brick, and before the December meeting the track was surfaced with three million ten-pound bricks. The programmes on the May, July and September public holidays were well attended. Nevertheless, it was decided to hold, in 1911, just one race of 500 miles for the unprecedentedly large purse of $25,000, and such has been the programme ever since, except during the war years 1916–8 and 1942–5.

Since the corners are so few and so similar, manoeuvrability is unimportant on the speedway and, although the ability to corner fast is indeed valuable, a very large improvement in cornering power is needed to overtake a car which has entered a corner on the right line. Thus places are gained largely by acceleration, by the brakes and the engine and, because the race is so long, the engine must have not only a generous torque curve but also endurance.

Thus the race has always been regarded as principally an engine-builders' contest; a good racing engine can win in a chassis which would be out-classed in a road race, but never has an indifferent engine won. As an extreme illustration, Harry Stutz entered in the first '500' the very first Stutz car ever built; using the proved Wisconsin engine it finished eleventh, although with only 390 cubic inches displacement compared to the allowable maximum of 600 c.i.d.

In 1912 the present limit of 35 starters was introduced. Next year the maximum capacity was reduced

RALPH HEPBURN   LEON DURAY   ANTHONY GULOTTA.

Norman Batten's Car on Fire.

to 450 c.i.d. to attract entries from Europe, and the race was won by a European car every year until 1920. In that year the 3 litre formula was adopted, a year before it took effect internationally, but the race was won by Gaston Chevrolet in one of seven 4 cylinder Frontenac entries built by the Chevrolet brothers. Louis Chevrolet in a Frontenac eight won next year, and a Miller-engined Duesenberg in 1922. In 1923 engines were limited to 2 litres, again to Grand Prix formula, and Ford T models with Frontenac valve-in-head conversions appeared. In 1926 the new Grand Prix limit of 1½ litres was adopted; however, no European car qualified until Chiron brought the redoubtable straight-eight roller-bearing Delage in 1929, finishing seventh.

'Offy' Era

In 1929 the artificial boom created by centralized control of American banks collapsed, and Eddie Rickenbacker, who had bought the Speedway in 1927, raised the capacity limit to 6 litres and excluded supercharging, in order to allow stock car engines to compete in 1930. However, victory continued to lie with Miller straight-eights and fours, the four becoming in 1935 the Offenhauser which continued to dominate the circuit for 30 years.

In 1938 Grand Prix racing reverted to capacity limits; Indianapolis adopted the formula of 4½ litres, or 3 litres supercharged, and retained it even after supercharged engines were reduced to 1½ litres in international racing. A 3 litre Maserati won con-

vincingly in the hands of Wilbur Shaw in 1939 and 1940; in 1941 a big Offenhauser was first, but second place went to a supercharged straight-eight built by Ed Winfield. The same engineer designed a supercharged V-eight, known as the Novi, which, as might be expected, was substantially more powerful than the $4\frac{1}{2}$ litre fours. First in front-drive and then in rear-drive Kurtis chassis, the Novi demonstrated its ability to break records and to qualify fastest, but in the race they wore out tyres and, unluckily as many would say, did no better than fourth (1947) or third (1948).

In 1957 the rules changed, in the same proportions for all engines, to 4.2 litres, and 2.8 litres supercharged. Offenhauser fours and Novi eights were both reduced in size, some of the Offenhausers to 2.8 litres, but no new engines appeared until 1963.

Ford at 'The Brickyard'

When the Ford V-eight had first appeared, Miller had adopted it for his front-drive chassis, in which engine length was critical, and despite being only 3,622 c.c., four of the cars qualified in 1935. The 4.2 litre (256 c.i.d.) limit was smaller than the passenger car V-eights of the 'sixties, and in 1963 Ford returned to the '500' with an engine cast in aluminium, but closely similar to a stock engine, carburetted and running on petrol, mounted in a Lotus frame. The rear-engine configuration had not only the usual advantages of reduced inertia, increased weight transfer on to the driving wheels, and reduced frontal area because of the absence of a drive shaft passing the driver, but was particularly suited to the Speedway because the independent rear suspension facilitated tuning for the

68

Above
Indianapolis speedway from the air, with the cars lined up for the start.

Right
Rolling start for the 1965 race at Indianapolis. Jim Clark is on the left of the front row.

corners, whereas live axles had kept the wheels
parallel. On the first appearance of both engine and
chassis in the '500', the car finished an extremely close
second. In 1964 the Ford engines were unreservedly
performance power plant, with the inlet ports in
between the camshafts (necessitating fuel injection
because of the 45° inclination) and the exhaust ports
either above or below the heads for rear- or front-
engine installation. Although Ford-Lotus cars qualified fastest, rear-engined cars again did no better than
second, and Offenhauser engines filled every place
down to eleventh, a Novi. This year saw also another
momentous innovation, Ferguson-Formula four-
wheel-drive, which promised to exploit the power of
the Novi, but this car and two other V-eights, Ford-
powered Thompson and Halibrand chassis, were
eliminated in a disastrous crash on the first lap.

Next year the tables were turned, there being only
three Offenhauser engines and only two front-engine
cars in the first 10 places. In 1966 several of the Offenhausers were equipped with mechanical or turbine-
driven superchargers in order to match the performance of the 32 valve Fords, but nevertheless V-
eights took the first four places in Lola, Lotus,
Brabham and Gerhardt chassis.

Enter the Turbine

The only 4 cylinder engines to qualify in 1967 were
supercharged, but the innovation of the year was a
Ferguson-Formula car with a United Aircraft free-
turbine engine, arranged with the longitudinal drive
shaft in the backbone chassis, the engine on the left and
the driver on the right of the backbone. The gas
turbine car led comfortably up to 490 miles, when a
bearing in the engine gearcase filed, and Ford-engined
cars—a Coyote, Lola, Coyote, Eagle and Moore—
finished in that order ahead of it.

In 1968 the air intake annulus area of gas turbines
was reduced, but even so two United Aircraft engines
with two of the three axial compressor stages removed
qualified fastest in four-wheel-drive Lotus chassis.
However, one turbine car crashed and two suffered
engine failure immediately after a period of running at
reduced speed, and so at last a supercharged engine

USAC regulations do not allow variable aerofoils, (cars now have fixed foils) and restrict front wheels to narrow widths.

won. And at last the USAC admitted that the 3:2 ratio for normally-aspirated and supercharged engines rendered the unsupercharged engine uncompetitive. The Club could have restored the normally-aspirated engine to 4.5 litres, to which limit the Offenhauser engines had long been built. They could have introduced a third, smaller displacement limit for engines with turbo-charging. But instead they reduced all supercharged engines from 171 to 161 c.i.d.—a highly controversial change indeed, since it would be easily accomplished on the Offenhauser with head and cylinder casting separate from the crankcase, with very little effect on the power, but would be prohibitively expensive on the Novi with monobloc cylinders and crankcase. And indeed the Novi engine has been withdrawn, and turbo-superchargers have become standard.

Aerofoils

Very much the same story can be seen in the application of aerodynamics to the cars. The gas turbine car that was so nearly successful in 1967, used an air-brake to compensate for the lack of engine braking. And the USAC made a rule which prevented any variable aerofoils. Consequently, cars now have fixed aerofoils, which have indeed resulted in a major improvement in cornering power—in 1972 there was the unprecedented sight of cars cornering two or even three abreast—but which impose even more down-load at speed on the straights, resulting in a severely compromised suspension design and in reduced maximum speeds because of the unwanted drag.

Nor were these the only changes in the rules. In the same period that gas turbines and supercharged cars were being handicapped, USAC first restricted the front wheels to narrow tyres—four-wheel-drive cars had used wide tyres all round—and then excluded four-wheel-drive altogether. It is clear beyond doubt that the rules are being used to prevent any more of the dramatic changes which characterized the early 'sixties, when one owner pointed to his fleet of front-engine four-cylinder cars and said to the assembled reporters, 'Gentlemen, you are looking at a million dollars worth of junk!' The Speedway's customers are not engine manufacturers or tyre makers or chassis constructors, who would be eager to try out new developments but cannot risk their capital unless they know that they will have ample notice of any change in the rules. The Speedway is out to please the spectators, it works to fill the grid with closely matched cars so that the outcome depends upon the drivers and upon fortune.

Right
The Ferguson-Formula Novi-engined four-wheel-drive driven in 1964 and 1965 by Bobby Unser. This was comfortably the fastest car of the 4.2 litre—2.8 litre supercharged formula.

Below
1972 winner Donohue and Roger Penske's model Sunoco McLaren M16B (with a turbo-charged Offenhauser) after his Indy win.

Below right
Pit-stop for A. J. Foyt during the Indy 500.

Chapter 10

An End And A Beginning

French Grand Prix 1914

Brute force and extra litres had been the maxim in motor sport competition until about 1907; capacities had grown and grown and finally gone wild with machines of up to 18 litres. Fiats, for instance, the great motor racing victors of that year—had increased engine size from the first-listed 6 h.p. Corsa with a 1,082 c.c. unit, to a 3 litre car in 1901, over 6 litres in 1902, 10.6 litres the following year, 14 in 1904, and a giant 16,286 c.c. Gordon Bennett racing car in 1905—raising its output from 110 b.h.p. to 130 for the Grand Prix de France Corsa car in 1907. Most other marques made this capacity climb with them until the grids were packed with monstrous top-heavy metal.

But voiturette racing had also made its mark; by this time the monsters were often capable of being soundly beaten by much lighter cars. It was time to think again about the old principle of 'bigger engines, more power'. By 1908 a bore restriction of 155 mm brought about some—though not enough—change in capacity. During the following few years racing quietly wilted, to be revived by a new *Formula Libre* in 1912. But not before Bugatti had entered a tiny 1.3 litre car in the previous year's Grand Prix, astonishing everyone by capturing a second place. The 1912 race was also significant particularly for its most advanced entrant, a Peugeot designed by Swiss engineer, Henry,

Hurried pit stop for Wagner's Mercedes during the 1914 French Grand Prix.

Left
The 1907 and 1908 French
Grands Prix were run on a
48-mile circuit outside Dieppe.
By 1908 a bore restriction had
come into force, leading, by
1914, to an engine-size
restriction of 4.5 litres. Here an
artist illustrates a lively Opel in
the 1908 event.

who, with French driver Georges Boillot, believed
that the giants of the track had outlived their day.

The Peugeot had a 16 valve 4 cylinder unit with
twin overhead camshafts; there were two varieties, the
Coupe de l'Auto car of 3 litres and the Grand Prix car of
7.7 litres. With the latter Boillot won the Grand Prix,
run concurrently with the smaller car race. Boillot's
win with a new French car elevated him to the status of
a national hero that year.

In 1913 the French Grand Prix was run on the
Circuit de Picardy, near Amiens, and this again was
won by Georges Boillot in a twin-cam Peugeot, now
reduced to 5.6 litres. Boillot was again fêted by the
crowds as a sporting hero.

It was not surprising, therefore, that when the 1914
French Grand Prix, to be held at the Lyons circuit on
July 4, was announced, Boillot and his Peugeot were
hot favourites. The year itself was also significant.
Nationalism and pride in national prowess was at its
height; and European countries were already uneasy,
feeling the threat of wars and calamities closing in
since the heir to the Austro-Hungarian empire had
fallen victim to an assassin's gun.

It was a packed Grand Prix entry, and one that even
those who only casually came to watch felt was either
the beginning of something different in motor racing,
or the end of an epoch. In fact it was both—the last
major race of what could be called pioneering days,
only a few months away from the most terrible war
history had ever seen; and the beginning of a new type
of race, in which team tactics were to play a vital role
in securing victory.

All the big names were there, Mercedes, Sunbeam,
Fiat, Delage, Schneider, Vauxhall, Opel—39 competitors, including 13 works teams. And each car was new,
designed for the race. The Peugeots had four-wheel
brakes and streamlining, the 4.5 litres Mercedes units
were based on aero engines, wire wheels were seen on
almost all cars, many had overhead valves, some four
valves per cylinder and five-speed boxes. All the
'international' drivers were present—Szisz, Nazarro,
Gabriel, Ralph de Palma, Lautenschlager, Wagner,
K. Lee Guinness—names that were already legends in
the motor racing world.

They started in pairs at half-minute intervals. Fifth
away was Boillot, paired with a Schneider. Ninety
seconds later the first of the Mercedes took off with
Sailer at the wheel. The French spectators were restless.
They wanted their man to get round the first lap of the
466 mile race ahead of the field—and indeed the first
car to whip down the shallow hill towards *Les Sept
Chemins* and the stands was Boillot himself in the blue

Left
Grand Prix de France 1912.
One of the last of the monsters,
the Fiat 574. This one, with
over 14 litres of engine
capacity, was driven by Louis
Wagner into second place—
behind a Peugeot of half the
size piloted by Boillot.

Right
The French favourite Georges
Boillot in his 1913 Peugeot.

Peugeot. The locals went wild with delight. They were more subdued a few minutes later when Sailer appeared. Rapid mental mathematics told them that although Boillot was first geographically, the Mercedes had lapped in 21 minutes 11 seconds—18 seconds faster than the Frenchman.

On the second lap Sailer stayed in front on lap times, though again Boillot actually led. And George Boillot intended to be in the lead in both senses. He trod on the boards. The race began to look like a four-cornered contest, with a Delage and a Sunbeam lying in wait for the leaders to drive themselves into the ground. When the Mercedes actually appeared on the Peugeot's tail, the great French driver was stung into even greater effort. He took his car up to speeds of 116 m.p.h. on the straights and fought crazily round bends, trusting that his four-wheel brakes would give

him the last inch of advantage over the two-wheel anchors of the German car.

Behind them three other team Mercedes ran in a loose convoy, laced between the leading British car and the Delage, waiting for something to happen. When Boillot called into the pits for another set of tyres—two plain, two steel-studded—Sailer slipped into the lead. The Frenchman, hopping mad by this time, chased off after him at a burning pace.

Lap five saw the Mercedes out of the race—Sailer's car had grated to a halt with a broken crankshaft. The roar of the crowd could be heard above the engines' scream as Boillot's number went up on the board as leader once again.

But the damage had been done to the Frenchman's chances, and the German team knew it, for this was precisely what had been planned at the team's closely guarded pre-race conferences. Lautenschlager peeled off the Mercedes convoy and began to harras Boillot. Slowly the distance between the two cars was whittled down. The rest of the field seemed mere shadows against the drama of this high-speed tactical warfare.

On the tenth lap Christian Lautenschlager turned his car into the replenishment pits for fuel. The positions were now first Boillot, Wagner (Mercedes), Salzer (Mercedes) and Goux in the second Peugeot. A few laps later, the team opened out to let Lautenschlager through again into second place with the smooth precision of a routine exercise.

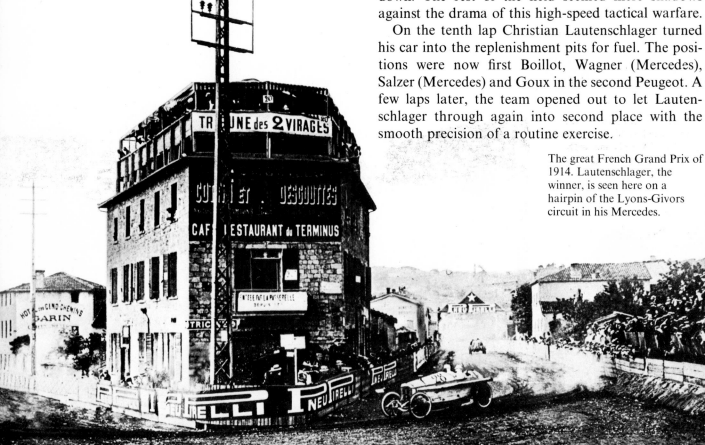

The result of the 1914 Grand Prix was by then predictable. Boillot called briefly into the pits, Lautenschlager called into the pits; the Mercedes continued to hound the Peugeot. It became an affair of honour, a duel of national prides, an ominous shadow of what was soon to happen in grim earnest between France and Germany and the rest of the world.

Just twelve miles before the finish Boillot's car began to plunge and rattle and shake. The Peugeot began to slow down; Boillot's lead dropped to a few seconds, to a few metres—then the Mercedes was past, Lautenschlager (so it was later learned) so intent on driving through the blinding dust and gravel that he saw nothing of the crippled French car. It was the end of the race for the Peugeot, which came to a forlorn stop on the side of the track, its differential shattered. Lautenschlager ploughed on faster, still searching for Boillot, and in fact passed the winner's flag without realizing that he had won the race . . .

The 1914 Grand Prix was a triumph for the meticulously prepared Mercedes, a triumph of team tactics (the racing world learned much that day) and it had been the most internationally attended race ever seen. It convinced the motor industry—despite Boillot's failure—that four-wheel brakes were a necessity, although they were slow to put the lesson into practice.

79

Threshold of Today
Monaco 1959

Right
1959 Monaco line-up. Front row, from the right: Moss, Behra, Brabham. The start-line has since been moved, and the houses have grown taller since those days.

Centre right
. . . the gasworks have gone, too, which no-one much regrets. This was Gasworks hairpin in 1959.

This Grand Prix ushered in the new Formula One rear-engine design—the first of the designs that developed into the Grand Prix cars of the present. It had all been done before, of course, when Auto-Union had put their engine behind the driver, but then nobody had followed the lead. Rob Walker's Coopers, driven by Stirling Moss and Maurice Trintignant had started the trend again by defeating the front-engined field in Argentina and Monaco the previous year, and now Jack Brabham was to set the seal of the success of the small rear-engined Coopers, leading Formula One into its present layout, as well as driving to his first World Championship that year.

The photographs show the atmosphere of Grand Prix racing of the late 'fifties and early 'sixties, when Tony Brooks, Jean Behra and Phil Hill drove for Ferrari and the BRMs were conducted by Bonnier and American Harry Schell. In 1959 Graham Hill drove a front-engined Lotus of uncertain habits; Moss drove a Cooper—and was unlucky most of the time. In 1959 the start at Monaco was in front of the harbour stand; the Gasworks were still there, the sky-scrapers were but an architect's nightmare. At Monaco in 1959 the smallest chip in the Casino was two (new) francs, a blow-out lunch cost ten, and a room almost next to the Palace could cost as little as £1. Tyres were thinner, drivers were still visible, the cars were $2\frac{1}{2}$ litres, and we were all very young . . .

Right
A cool and quiet walk in the holiday season, the tunnel is a whirlpool of noise during the Grand Prix.

Below
Newcomers to Monte Carlo may not recognize this corner either—Station Bend is without a railway station now. Here Brooks (Ferrari) follows Trintignant (Cooper-Climax) through the tight corner.

Above
View from the wheel. Stirling Moss lines his car up for the chicane.

The Changing Shape of Racing

The pictures speak for themselves. From the earliest days of the sport when the shape of a car was dictated by what you hung on the 'Christmas Tree', the frame, through the first clumsy streamlining (the architecture was usually perpendicular then), to the present Formula cars whose designers seem dedicated to making drivers invisible and cars almost two-dimensional, the shape of racing vehicles has constantly been changing as engineering and engineers have become more sophisticated . . .

Above
Advanced Opel, 1913, with slightly less to present to the wind.

Above right
Although the 250 F Maserati of the '50s was not a sophisticated car, its body-shape is generally acknowledged to be the zenith of design aesthetics. It really *looked* like a Grand Prix vehicle.

Left
Uncompromisingly upright, the 1902 Fiat *Corsa*.

Below
This 1929 4½ litre supercharged Bentley shows the traditional line of the period.

Right
Formula 1 Ferrari. Rear engines had taken over, and cars were built nearer the ground by the time this 1.5 litre car showed its nostrilled nose in 1961.

Below
In the late '60s they grew high stabilizing wings. By 1970 these had developed into a more solid aerofoil close behind the driver's head, and fins had appeared at the front end.

Below right
Today's shape in Grand Prix racing.

Chapter 11

Dad's Heroes

The Sport Between The Wars

Europe was slow to shake off the dust and debris of war. The 1914–18 conflagration had shaken nations to their foundations—particularly France, leader of the world of motoring, and Germany, founder country of the automobile. Roads had been blasted into pock-marked mud tracks, towns had vanished. The car had proved its worth as transport and as a war machine; there was much painful rebuilding to do before it could be thought of as a sporting vehicle once again. It was 1921 before circuit racing was revived.

Perhaps the simplest way to follow motor sport history between the two World Wars is by looking at the changes of Formulae under which Grand Prix races were won and, at the time of each change, at the drivers and cars dominating the scene. Grand Prix racing in 1921 was run much as it is today, under a Formula set by the International authority originally known as the AIACR (Association Internationale des Automobile Club Reconnus) and now as the FIA (Fédération Internationale de l'Automobile).

By 1921 the old $4\frac{1}{2}$ litre Formula had given way to 3 litres with an 800 kg minimum weight rule. The first race was the French Grand Prix held in July over a very rough circuit of 10.6 miles at Le Mans. The hero of the year was an American, Jimmy Murphy, who won the race in a Duesenburg, the first-ever American

'Bunny', the famous wooden-spoked Aston Martin, at Brooklands during a record run. In 1922 this car took 10 world and 22 class records. The driver here is S. C. H. (Sammy) Davis, third from the left, adjusting his goggles.

Left
The start of a voiturette
Grand Prix at Brescia, 1923.
Circuit racing had been revived
two years earlier.

Above
A pit stop for the 3 litre
Sunbeam at Le Mans, 1925,
with S. C. H. Davis holding
the can. This twin-overhead
camshaft car, driven by Davis
and Chassagne, took the car to
second place at this race.

Grand Prix car equipped with hydraulic four-wheel
brakes. An American win in this first post-war Grand
Prix has its own niche in history, as it was something
not to be repeated for many years—although Murphy
went on to win the Indianapolis 500 with the car (fitted
with a Miller power unit) the following year.

By 1922 the Formula had been reduced to a 2 litre
limit, which stayed in force until 1924. It was during
this period that the Italian manufacturers, notably
Alfa Romeo, began to be seen in the ascendant. For
the British there was a notable event in 1923 when
Segrave (after lying fifth most of the way, held back
with clutch trouble) won the French Grand Prix in a
Sunbeam, a rare victory for a British driver in a
British car—a 'double' not repeated until Tony
Brooks driving a Connaught, won the Syracuse Grand
Prix in 1955.

It was also in this period that the Bugatti became a
serious contender, particularly when the Type 35,
with its aluminium wheels, fine engineering and
impeccable performances appeared in 1926. In 1925
there had been a considerable change in the Grand
Prix scene, since riding mechanics, who up to that
time had always been carried, were barred, even though
the mechanic's seat remained an obligation. Since
there was nobody to tell the driver what was going on

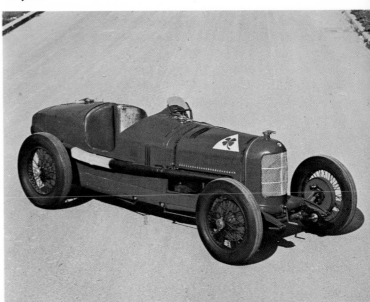

behind him a driving mirror became obligatory. It was taken as something of a slight by a small number of drivers, who refused to admit that it could ever be necessary to be on the lookout for an overtaking car!

By 1926 speeds had increased and Grand Prix regulations had shrunk engine sizes to $1\frac{1}{2}$ litres (even Indianapolis followed suit in this, giving birth to the famous Miller '91') and a number of very exciting cars were produced as a result, particularly a straight-eight $1\frac{1}{2}$ litre Delage with twin superchargers which first appeared in 1926 to take first at Brooklands, and four Grands Prix in 1927. Others with interesting new cars were Bugatti (Type 39), Talbot, Alvis, and Itala (whose design was rather too novel for the time, and which never raced).

However, few manufacturers made cars that would fit into the $1\frac{1}{2}$ litre Formula, and that, coupled with the

official ending of the 1½ litre regulations in December 1927, produced five years of free-for-all racing. There was, in fact, an official Formula which stated that cars should be between 550 and 750 kg, with unrestricted engine size; this was ignored by most and a completely free Formula was adopted.

It was certainly a period of triumph for Ettore Bugatti, who sold his cars to private owners. At least on one occasion a Grand Prix was started with 14 cars on the grid, 13 of which were Bugattis. This doldrum period was also turned to excellent effect by the Alfa Romeo Company, who tried a number of ingenious designs, many of which were to pay off at a later date.

The 750 Formula

The first genuine Grand Prix milestone in the 1930s occurred in 1934 with the introduction of an international Formula limiting the weight of the cars to 750 kilogrammes (with no restriction on the size of the engine and only a limitation on the frontal area of the car to decide the shape of the body). This Formula produced the Monoposto Alfa Romeo, one of the classic racing cars of all time which, particularly in the hands of Tazio Nuvolari ('Brakes are no good, they only make you go slower'), swept all before it. Nuvolari was certainly the most exciting figure of the

period and became a legend well within his lifetime. He had a way of hurling his car round corners which not only defied description but appeared, at least at that time, to defy most natural laws as well.

The extent of Nuvolari's prowess is perhaps best measured when a few years later, after the Germans had introduced their all-conquering Mercedes and Auto-Union cars, he managed (at a German Grand Prix of all occasions) to beat the lot of them by sheer driving ability. But, apart from the immortal Tazio, the Hitler-sponsored German cars were so far ahead of the opposition that they became virtually unbeatable. They also produced a race of hero-drivers including Rosemeyer, Brauchitsch, Caracciola (a German in spite of his Italian name) and one notable Englishman, Richard Seaman.

Two 'byeways' of this period are worth noting; the first, the 1,500 c.c. voiturette races which had sprung into prominence when the rest of the world, sick of trailing behind the Germans, had decided to have some racing fun in a different category. This movement was largely led by Maserati, followed by the British who, without any hope of being able to enter the Grand Prix scene, had some notable successes with the ERA in this light-car sport. The ERA project, financed by Humphrey Cook, and with the assistance of Raymond

Mays as a driver, and Peter Berthon as designer, began to enjoy considerable fame. Against the weight of the ERAs was ranged a single British independent, Richard Seaman, who had bought a 10 year-old Delage, and having rebuilt it with the assistance of Ramponi, succeeded in scoring no less than four firsts in the 1936 season, gaining an invitation from team manager Neubauer to drive for Mercedes.

As has happened so often before, the power and speed of the Grand Prix cars of the day horrified the sport's authorities. It is difficult today to appreciate the dangers of the 400-plus brake horsepower unleashed in these monsters; advanced as they were by the standards of their day, neither suspension nor tyres had a tenth of the sophistication of those of today, and on anything less than a gentle curve, a car could often be seen careering sideways with the driver's arms twisted up like spaghetti as he applied opposite lock. It was not surprising therefore that in 1938 the Formula was restricted to what was, in effect, 3 litres, in the fond hope that this would reduce the speed of the cars. It in fact did no such thing, but with slightly lighter and more manageable vehicles, driving techniques improved.

In 1938–9 the Mercedes 3 litre W154 and W163 represented the ultimate in design, producing 483 b.h.p. at 7,800 r.p.m. Power units were V12s with four valves per cylinder. The cars won nine major events in the '38 and '39 seasons, driven by Lang, Brauchitsch, Caracciola and Richard Seaman.

The scene constantly changes and shifts over the years, changes marked by new drivers, new Formula regulations, by more advanced driving techniques, better metals and machinery, improved tyres, suspension systems, road surfaces, new safety regulations. Perhaps the most noticeable non-technical change since the green days before World War II is commercial sponsorship, without which racing today would have been several years less advanced and many private purses more slender. The inter-war years were certainly more 'sportive', more gentlemanly and amateur, and contemporaries look back with fondness, and sometimes a little sadness, at the long-gone days of Nuvolari, Caracciola, Seaman; of Fiats on the circuit, of Bugs and Bentleys and Auto-Union, of the colours—silver for Germany, green for Britain (they called it England then), of blazing Italian red and French blue—at the days when motor racing was fun—for everyone . . .

Chapter 12

Third Generation

At the turn of the century motor sport was in its infancy; the period was followed by what could be called the second generation of cars—before the second war—when names like Auto-Union and Mercedes Benz were on every lip. But after World War II the generation gap was larger than ever before. There were three basic reasons for this. First was the six-year gap of the war years themselves; secondly the great technological advances brought about by the emergency, and finally the further time needed after the war, to incorporate the new technical know-how into new models.

Among drivers, too, there was a generation gap. Famous names like Rosier and Etancelin were still around, and the Monagasque Louis Chiron was still to win the Monte Carlo Rally in a Lancia; but by 1950 new names were also claiming recognition. Twenty five years earlier Antonio Ascari had been a great driver with Alfa Romeo, but now his son Alberto (with the same marque) was getting the attention. In 1948 he started to climb to fame when he finished third in the French Grand Prix in an Alfa Romeo, but was later linked with the great name of Ferrari.

The V12 Ferrari which Alberto Ascari drove with such skill in the late 'forties was a formidable machine indeed, with twin-overhead camshafts on each bank

The 158 Alfa Romeo; its 1479 c.c. 8 cylinder unit gave almost 200 b.h.p. at 7,500 r.p.m. in its original form in 1938, and in 1950, eighteeen years later, with power raised to 360 b.h.p., it took Farina to the World Championship title.

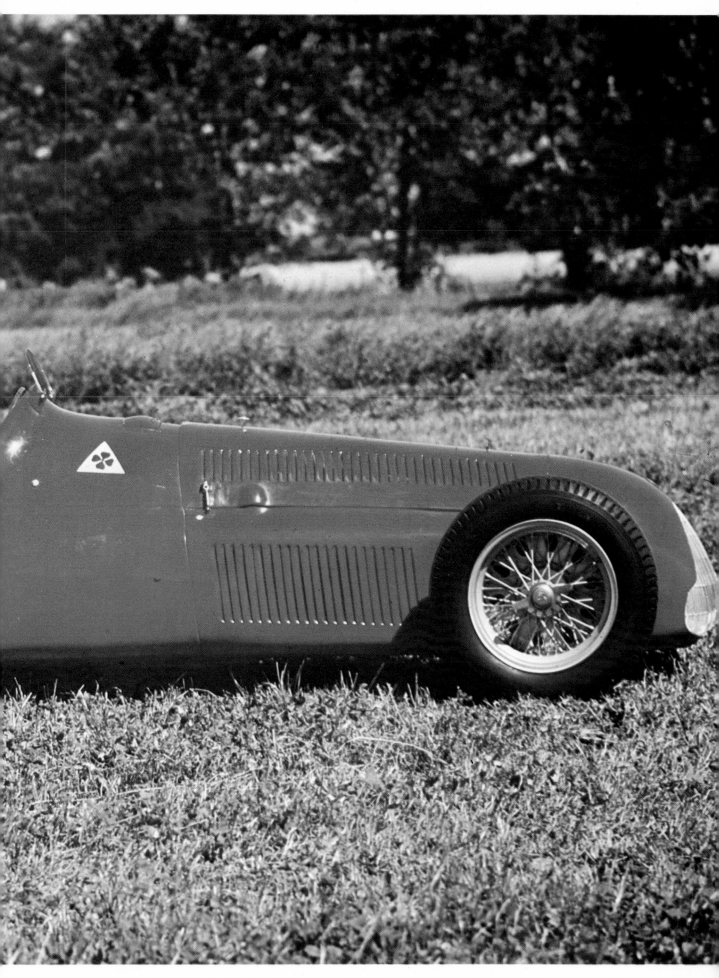

of cylinders, transverse leaf springs all round with double wishbones at the front and swing axles at the rear (an interesting design, for leaf springs have a weight disadvantage) and two-stage supercharging to over 30 lb. per sq. in.; the engine developing 314 b.h.p. at something over 7,500 r.p.m. Ascari himself became a supreme driver—he was World Champion in 1952 and 1953—but after a miraculous escape in the 1955 Monaco Grand Prix, when he plunged into the harbour, he was killed during a test drive in Italy.

In April, 1950, 'Casque' (an alias of S. C. H. Davis, racing driver and former editor of 'Autocar') commented in his journal on the new generation of drivers. While, with the lack of instructional tracks like Brooklands, it was harder to learn the techniques and the cost problem was greater, said Davis, there were still plenty of promising drivers. He singled out one from a family interested in motor sport and equestrian events, a young man with a style of his own. This man drove really fast, he understood how a car should be taken round a corner, continuing unchecked where so many others cut off. Casque commented that to do this without wild skidding, and to accept misfortune philosophically, were further good points. He was writing after the driver's string of successes in 500 c.c. (Formula Three) racing—his name, Stirling Moss.

Left
Famous names such as Phillipe Etancelin were still around . . . here seen in a Talbot in 1949.

Above
Guiseppe Farina in the Type 158 Alfa Romeo at Silverstone, 1950.

Below left
July 1953; the start of the race that most present claimed to be the greatest they had ever seen—the French Grand Prix, won by the Ferrari 'apprentice' Mike Hawthorn.

Right
French Grand Prix 1953; a scene from the stands as a Ferrari and a Maserati trail the leaders down the straight at Rheims.

And what a great deal the 500 c.c. category and the original one-mile kidney shaped track at Brands Hatch, Kent, did for coming drivers in those days. The crackle of a Cooper, at first with JAP engine and later Norton, was part of the stimulating small-car racing scene, leading in time to a predominance of British drivers in the world racing picture.

The Airfield Circuit

On 13 May 1950, the first European Grand Prix ever to be run in Britain took place at the new track made from a converted wartime airfield at Silverstone, in the Midlands. The weather was perfect and the crowd was estimated at some 120,000, including a Royal party headed by King George VI. With the Ferrari team absent, the Type 158 Alfa Romeos were expected to win at this early 'third generation' event; and indeed the event was won by the immaculate stylist Guiseppe Farina. His team-mate, the legendary-to-be Juan Manuel Fangio, retired with a broken oil pipe. At that time, successful non-Italian cars such as Cooper-Climax and Lotus were not even on the drawing board, and at this 1950 Silverstone meeting most of the excitement lay farther back in the field with the veteran

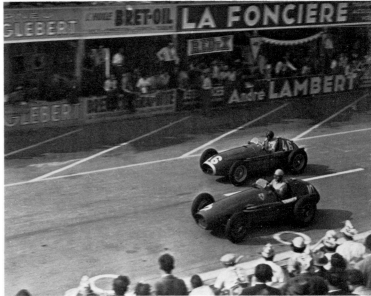

ERAs of Bob Gerard and Cuth Harrison, two drivers who enlivened many a race meeting in those years with their wheel-to-wheel racing, and in this race there were just two-fifths of a second between them at the finish after 200 miles! However, there was a promise for a British future in the demonstration run by Raymond Mays of the advanced but ill-fated V16 1½ litre supercharged BRM.

For British racegoers a highlight in this rather special year of 1950 happened in August when it was announced that the immortal Tazio Nuvolari, often given the title of the greatest driver of them all, was to drive in the production car race at Silverstone at the Daily Express Trophy meeting. Sadly his health was failing and he could not take part. However, thousands of a new generation of British enthusiasts were able to see at least the great little man in the flesh.

The Trophy race itself provided the disappointment of the decade for the crowds. The much-publicized BRM V16 cars ran into pre-race trouble, and at the last moment one car only was flown to the circuit and allowed to qualify late by special permission. This was supposed to be a great day for the car but, as the starter's flag fell, Raymond Sommer was left at the line with a failed transmission—the first of a long series of troubles for the new marque. Farina and Fangio, both driving Alfa Romeos, were respectively in first and second places.

The fortunes of Grand Prix motor racing change rapidly, and by 1953 Ferrari and Maserati were the names to conjure with, also-rans being Gordini, Cooper-Bristol, Connaught and HWM. In the sports car field Jaguar were on top, but the Cunningham from the USA was really having a try, and from France the Talbot was to be reckoned with.

The Greatest Grand Prix?

In July '53 came the race which everyone present claimed to be the greatest they had ever seen; something they felt would never be equalled for drama. This was the French Grand Prix, held at Rheims.

It was preceded by the 12 hour sports car race which, although won for Jaguar by a magnificent drive by Stirling Moss, proved on the day to be but a curtain raiser. In the Press Box, seasoned journalists of publications like 'Autocar', 'Motor' and 'L'Equipe' for once gave up any attempt to keep their usually impeccable lap-charts, and during the tense 30 laps before the end all press activity ceased as the cars were watched in silent awe.

This Grand Prix was run under the Formula Two category for 2 litre cars, the main contenders being the Maseratis of the great Fangio and his countryman Gonzalez, and the Ferraris of Ascari, Farina, Villoresi

and the young Englishman Mike Hawthorn. After 60 laps—311.22 miles—four cars crossed the finish line with fewer than five seconds between them. In sixth place was Villoresi, fifth was Farina and fourth Ascari (Ferraris), and then in third place the Maserati of Gonzalez; but the heartstopping duel was between Fangio's Maserati and the comparative new boy Hawthorn in his Ferrari. This lasted throughout the last half of the race with the cars bonnet-to-bonnet at the end of each lap. The result: Hawthorn *one second*

ahead of Fangio, Gonzalez *four-tenths* of a second behind Fangio, and Ascari 3.2 seconds after Gonzalez. Having beaten in open combat the cream of the world's drivers, the blonde Mike Hawthorn was mobbed by the crowds.

The year 1955 gave the sport the greatest disaster on the track—at Le Mans—and the greatest Mille Miglia win—by Stirling Moss.

At Le Mans, British driver Lance Macklin's Austin-Healey had pulled out to pass Hawthorn's Jaguar,

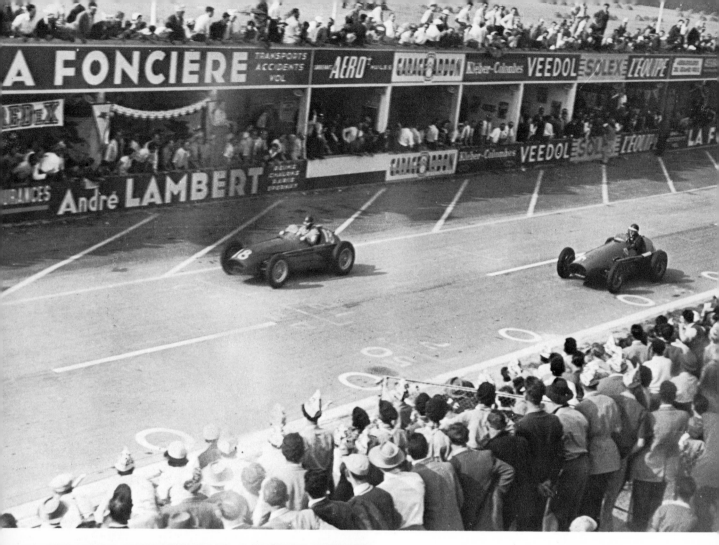

calling at the pits, and was struck by Pierre Levagh's Mercedes which was travelling flat out down the straight at around 150 m.p.h. In a split second the Healey was a wreck and the Mercedes had flown into the crowd in front of the main stands. A cloud of smoke went up into the ironically blue sky, obscuring the track for drivers as the yellow danger flags started waving, and more than 80 people lay dead or dying. The disaster gave rise to the policy of separating the pits from the track—at Le Mans and elsewhere.

A singularly poignant aspect of the Le Mans tragedy was that Levagh had been the hero of the crowds that day. Three years previously he had driven a $4\frac{1}{2}$ litre Talbot-Lago in the Le Mans race, and against almost invincible competition from Mercedes held the lead for hours in a mammoth *solo* drive. On the Sunday morning his tachometer failed and later the crankshaft started to break up. With fifty minutes of the race left, the engine failed. So, on the day of the 1955 disaster, at the wheel of a Mercedes himself, he would have been the most popular of winners. His last act was to raise his arm to warn his team-mate Fangio driving behind him of the impending disaster.

The Moss Mille Miglia

The 1955 Mille Miglia of 1955 was one of the highlights of the decade. This was the last to be run under the

traditional 'format' of a single 1,000 (Roman) miles' lap of Italy from Brescia to Vicenza, Padua, Rimini, Ancona, Pescara, then across the mountains to Rome and up through Florence, Bologna, Modena, Reggio, Palma, Mantua and back to Brescia. Moss and Fangio were driving the latest Mercedes Benz 300 SLR cars— Fangio alone, Moss with Jenkinson as navigator, 'Jenks' being equipped with a roll of paper from which he could signal to the driver the nature of each bend or corner as it came up.

The records bear witness to the skill of the astonishing Moss. He increased the past highest average speed by some 10 m.p.h., covering a thousand-mile lap at nearly 100 m.p.h. He was the first-ever British driver to win. He was the first-ever to have been leading at Rome (the legend that *he who led at Rome could never win the race* had been proved time and time again) and still won the race. And he left the great Fangio in a similar car more than half an hour behind at the finish. The race was described to British readers as equivalent to leaving London at 07.15, getting to Aberdeen by lunchtime, and back to London in time for a late tea—and with only two stops. It was little wonder that at the end of the race Moss, utterly exhausted, had to be lifted from the car and half carried away!

Chapter 13

Rallying And Why

On the face of it a motor rally is a curious kind of competition—neither fish, flesh, fowl nor good motor racing. In the beginning, however, it made much more sense. Rallying as a sport derived from the long-distance races such as the Paris-Vienna event of 1902, when competitors were allowed a number of night stops during the competition, and from the reliability trials of even earlier.

The first to organize a successful series of modern-type rallies were the ingenious Monagasques. The *Rallye Automobile Monte Carlo* is now one of the most distinguished and popular—if not the most sportive, in terms of driving difficulty—events in the calendar.

Some three years before World War I, the good people of Monaco, finding their hotel beds rather emptier than was good for trade, cast about for an event to attract a greater number of January visitors.

It was at first difficult to envisage any kind of event which could take place within or near the borders of the pocket principality, but, prompted by an Italian event known as the 'Convegni Ciclisti' in which competitors started from points all over Europe and made their way to a common destination, the President of the Automobile and Cycle Club of Monaco announced a rally in which competitors, who were to be private owners and members of recognized clubs, were

Modern Monte Carlo—a French Alpine screeches to a stop at a country control-point with book held out to be stamped.

invited to start from various points in Europe and drive to Monte Carlo—in a word to 'rally' there.

The first event was arranged in 1911 and was open to cars of any size, power or weight. The prize money was substantial, ranging from £8 to £400, and the competitors were free to start at a time of their own choosing, having an allowance of up to seven days to drive to Monte Carlo. The original starting points were Paris, Boulogne, Madrid, Rome, Berlin, Vienna, Brussels, Amsterdam, Geneva, Lisbon and St. Petersburg, and the average speed required was something like $15\frac{1}{2}$ miles an hour, calculated to allow for what were then considered normal stops. The winner was Henri Rougier in a Turcat Méry who drove from Paris to Monaco in 28 hours 10 minutes.

The Great War interfered with the continued running of the 'Monte' and it was not restarted until

1924 when, because both roads and motor cars had progressed considerably, the schedules were much tighter. This tightening-up process continued right up to the outbreak of World War II, rallies getting progressively more difficult—although in fact right up to that time they were more of a map-reading adventure than the ruthless, commercial-prestige competitions, which large international rallies have now become.

One of the first nations to mount a national rally was Great Britain—naturally enough, since the Monte Carlo Rally had originally attracted a great many British competitors—and in the 1930s the RAC mounted a rally of their own, which was (by today's standards) nothing more than a gentle junket with a series of driving tests at the end of it.

With improved driving techniques and advancing vehicle sophistication it had become reasonably easy to get to Monte Carlo on time in the 'thirties, and the organizers were faced with some kind of test which would sort out the real drivers from the 'boy racers'. This varied from ordinary driving tests on the sea front, to special regularity tests round the mountains, and in these tests the foundations of the future of the Monte Carlo Rally, and indeed all rallies, were laid.

After World War II the Monte Carlo Rally continued much as before, but with a number of special tests incorporated in the route on the way to Monte Carlo. These special stages on temporarily closed roads became progressively more difficult—more difficult in terms of road conditions themselves and more difficult to complete in the allotted time—and this time/difficulty factor has formed the basis of major rallies ever since.

The huge popularity of the Monte Carlo Rally with the British was no doubt behind the introduction of club rallies into that country after World War II—before which club sport had been centred around reliability trials in which competitors had to cover awkward terrain such as rutted and shaled hills, punctuated by limited-speed road sections. These had posed quite a different set of problems, ones which became obsolete as the cars improved.

A number of other countries began to organize rallies on a national scale, in the early post-war years among the most notable being the Tulip Rally organized from Holland, and the famous Liège-Rome-Liège event which, although it changed its nature a good deal during its life, became one of the most exciting and toughest events in the calendar. The Americans, too, have taken to rallying to some extent, although their rallies are predominantly timekeeping and navigational affairs in which the prize should un-

doubtedly go to the passenger rather than the driver.

Throughout the rest of the world, rallying has changed radically over the past decade. It has become a highly competitive sponsored event in which an entrant, to be successful, needs not only a good car, but a vast backing of service crews, and two or three weeks to reconnoitre the course before the event starts. This expensive preparation and service support has had the effect of reducing the number of private entrants in all international rallies (save perhaps Spain's Sherry Rally which remains predominantly an event for amateurs) almost to zero.

In Great Britain the club rally continues to prosper, and of all events the annual RAC Rally, held annually in November, manages best to bridge the gap between the professionals and the amateurs.

Over the past half century, then, rallying has slowly swung away from the assembly at a common point from starts either from another point or various ones scattered across a continent, with the difficulty of arriving at the finishing line in one piece the major hazard. Today only one event of this type is left—the East African Safari—an event which still draws the most adventurous. Occasionally super-rallies are mounted, such as the great trek from London, England to Sydney, Australia, and the London-Mexico Rally that was run at the same time as the World Cup football event, held in that country, but these are highly costly for the individual competitor

Above left
Rally equipment—night assistance. And heaven help the poor French motorist coming the other way . . .
Above
Meticulous work is needed at control points to prevent any of the thousand-and-one misunderstandings that can arise from a clerical error.

Right
East African Safari Rally, one of the toughest and most hazardous of all international rallies with its uncertain roads, its floods and its sometimes unfriendly wild-life. Here a Peugeot leaves the ground on a dusty bush road. Peugeots won this rally in 1966, '67 and '68.

and few true amateur drivers compete without some commercial support. 'Monte' type rallying, in which special speed-hazard stages, and perhaps a final run around mountain circuits at night finally decide the winner, is now the general pattern of European rallying.

Elsewhere some complaints are being heard from the non-rallying public—there just are not enough empty roads for cars to go chasing noisily around the countryside—and it may not be long before such events are driven off the road. Certainly a new image and a new form must eventually arrive; for special stages or closed roads have long been essential, and maybe rallies will some day be run entirely on such stages.

But whatever happens to rallying, the exhausting sport that seems to many—competitors included—to be at its most enjoyable when the cars have passed the finishing-line, there is one event that will never be forgotten—the great, colourful, controversial Monte Carlo Rally.

BRM Story

The name has always had a strong mystique. Even during the dismal days of the '50s when nothing went right, it was still defended by sports enthusiasts who considered it a uniquely British national product (many thought it was government-sponsored) and though some scornfully threw pennies into the cockpit when it was wheeled ignominiously back into the paddock, after failing to get off the grid at Silverstone in 1950, a hardcore of fans kept faith. They had to hang on to it for a considerable time, for it was 1959 before the BRM had a Grand Prix win. But by the end of the 1962 season it had taken Graham Hill to World Championship and secured the World Championship of Manufacturers for itself.

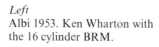

Left
Albi 1953. Ken Wharton with the 16 cylinder BRM.

Centre right
The V8 BRM in its early form in 1962, with upswept megaphone exhaust.

Below left
Silverstone 1965. Rear-engined since 1960, the 1½ litre V8 BRM by now had three full seasons of successful racing behind it.

Left
The 2½ litre front-engined BRM Type 25 at Silverstone in 1958, a year before its first Grand Prix victory. Flockhart at the wheel.

Below
Graham Hill joined the BRM organization in 1960 after a spell with Lotus, a car that at the time was almost as unreliable as the early Bourne products. With him is Raymond Mays, who with designer Peter Berthon, brought the BRM to life.

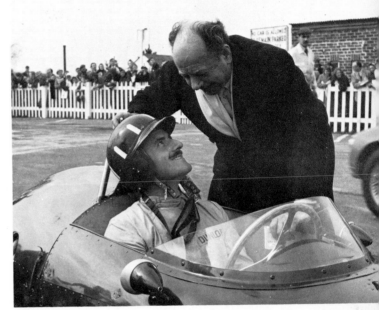

Below centre
Race of Champions, 1970. The V12 2998 c.c. here driven by George Eaton.

Below right
Peter Gethin takes the 1972 P180 440 b.h.p. BRM, now linked with Marlboro, round Druids at Brands Hatch. Designed by Tony Southgate this car was a semi-monocoque with a tubular rear sub-frame.

Chapter 14

The (All-American) Jet Set

In 1963 America's Craig Breedlove screamed across the Bonneville salt flats of Utah at more than 400 m.p.h. in his turbo-jet, Spirit of America. But because his car was not driven by its wheels his speed could not be recognized officially as the world land speed record. And since it had only three wheels it could not be classed as a car; officially it was a motorcycle!

Yet Breedlove said he didn't give a damn whether they recognized his feat or not; he was the fastest and the world knew it, and that was all that mattered. And with rivals building jet cars to challenge Breedlove, the FIA (Fédération Internationale de l'Automobile) realized that the time had come to rewrite the rules governing the record. Until this time it had been restricted to wheel-driven vehicles, but in 1964 came the change. Provided there was a driver aboard, the Land Speed Record would be open to any vehicle with four wheels on the ground. For the die-hards there would be a separate category for internal combustion engined wheel-driven vehicles called the World Record for Automobiles.

The jet age record breakers could go ahead, but the resources and logistics involved in raising the record were now so demanding that the record was to be a monopoly of American drivers at Bonneville.

The first jet age land speed record was credited to Art Arfons in 1964 who reached 434.20 m.p.h. in his

Land speed record holder Gary Gabelich, posing with the US Natural Gas Industry's *Blue Flame* with which he recorded 630.38 m.p.h. at Bonneville, Utah, in 1970.

Green Monster, a brutal torpedo looking like a grounded fighter aircraft and powered by a General Electric J79 engine of 17,500 b.h.p. Actually it was not green but red, white and blue! It was the first time the record had belonged to America since Ray Keech had taken it at less than half Arfon's speed in 1928.

Meanwhile, Art's older brother Walt was experimenting with a rocket-powered car, but this was not viable at the time.

Breedlove returned to Bonneville with a new four-wheeled Spirit of America, similarly styled to the Green Monster, with an aluminium and glass-fibre body, and similarly powered with a J79 turbojet from a Hustler bomber. He achieved 526.28 m.p.h.

Arfons retorted with 536.71 m.p.h. It was a duel in the tradition of Jenatzy and Chasseloup-Laubat, of Campbell and Segrave. And the record had been raised by more than 100 m.p.h. in a matter of months. The duel continued into 1965. Breedlove went to 555.10 m.p.h. and Arfons to 576.55. Eight days later—on 15 November 1965, Breedlove passed 600 m.p.h.

There, despite further attempts and dreams and schemes, the record remained until 1970, when Gary Gabelich, a 31-year-old drag racer and former test astronaut, came to the desert with the Blue Flame.

It was so called because it had been sponsored to the tune of half a million dollars by the American natural gas industry. Its rocket motor, similar to ones used in America's space programme, used liquefied natural gas and hydrogen peroxide as propellants, and delivered some 58,000 b.h.p.

The car itself looked like one of America's experimental rocket aircraft. It was 38 feet long—the longest record contender ever—with the cockpit immediately in front of the eight foot high tail fin. The front wheels were set so closely together that many observers thought they constituted one wheel of a tricycle undercarriage.

Five weeks of frustration followed as Gabelich pursued the record. Several times the fiery tail of his machine set fire to the cords of the parachutes that provided his ultimate braking power and the Blue Flame took 12 miles to stop. And then on 23 October, on his twenty-sixth run, Gary Gabelich travelled at 617.60 m.p.h. and 627.28 m.p.h. on the double run averaging 622.40 m.p.h.

Outside America the news of the new record received only a fraction of the publicity that was given to Parry Thomas and his Babs at Pendine sands back in the 'twenties.

And yet record breaking is probably more exacting, more dangerous than it has ever been. On one occasion Breedlove ran into the sea. In November 1966 Art Arfons and the Green Monster flipped 500 feet through the air and slid crazily for over a mile when he crashed at 610 m.p.h.

Within a week Arfons was back from hospital and in his workshops creating a new Monster to pass 300 m.p.h. from standstill in six seconds and which was theoretically capable of reaching 1,000 m.p.h.

That is the new target figure—1,000 m.p.h., though first must come the breaking of the sound barrier at 700 m.p.h. plus. And yet most people have still not exceeded 100 m.p.h. in a car.

Breaking the land speed record has become fantastically expensive. It took an industry rather than a firm to make the Gabelich record possible. But as long as there are records there will be men wanting to break them, men who want to be the fastest in the world.

Some key dates and names in the establishment of land speed records by jet cars

1964	A. Arfons (Green Monster)	434.20 m.p.h.
1964	C. Breedlove (Spirit of America)	526.28 m.p.h.
1964	A. Arfons (Green Monster)	536.71 m.p.h.
1965	C. Breedlove (Spirit of America)	555.10 m.p.h.
1965	A. Arfons (Green Monster)	576.55 m.p.h.
1965	C. Breedlove (Spirit of America)	600.60 m.p.h.
1970	G. Gabelich (Blue Flame)	622.41 m.p.h.

Left
Blue Flame at speed during its
record run at Bonneville.

Right
Officials chair Craig Breedlove
in triumph after his record of
468.72 m.p.h. (also at
Bonneville) on 13 October
1964. Two days later he pushed
the record up to 526.28 m.p.h.
—and had to swim from his
car when it wound up in an
18 ft. pool of brine!

Below
Breedlove's record run in the
three-wheeled Spirit of America
15 October 1964.

Chapter 15

Today's Men–Today's Cars

Motor racing has changed almost beyond recognition in recent years—and the pace of change is still accelerating. The emergence of Britain as the dominant motor racing nation in the late 'fifties changed the language of the pits from German, Spanish and Italian to English, but today the sport is more international than ever before.

The Championship-winning Cooper cars brought about the rear-engine revolution and led to almost identical layouts. The 1.5 litre Formula One of the 'sixties brought monocoque construction in place of space frames, to give rigidity and low weight. Tyres got bigger and wider, but cars got smaller and lower, and drivers were forced to adopt an almost recumbent position. Arms and elbows disappeared from view; only the drivers' helmets remained visible and they, too, became more enveloping. With the system of national colours for cars in disuse, the quickest identification of cars travelling at 170 m.p.h. became by the colour of the helmets—almost a return of the system of identification by jockeys' smocks worn by drivers at Brooklands at the start of the century.

Inevitably cars became faster, the 1.5 litre models lapping quicker than cars of double the engine size had done a few years earlier, but the number of companies producing Formula One engines shrank. The 3 litre

The late 1960s found most teams using identical Ford Cosworth engines . . . the notable exception was BRM, with a V12 unit.

ra
d
B
ri
w
C
ra
p
w
tu
w
st

J
A
d
C
d
th

p
In
M
d
th

Below
Italian Grand Prix 1972,
Emerson Fittipaldi in his John
Player Special garbed in the
rather funereal John Player
Team Lotus colours. The car
took Fittipaldi to the World
Championship in 1972.

Right
Yardley McLaren Ford M19A,
driven here by Peter Revson.

Centre right
Car for '72. The John Player
Special.

Below right
Cutting it fine at Druid's Bend,
Brands Hatch.

Emerson Fittipaldi

When the Brazilian became World Champion in 1972 at the age of 25 he was the youngest man to have won the title. But then his whole career justifies the over-worked adjective, 'meteoric'. Son of a racing journalist, he was a karting champion and then Formula Vee champion in Brazil before he travelled to England in 1969 in the wake of his older brother Wilson. He had just enough money for a Formula Ford car, from which he graduated to one of the Formula Three cars of Jim Russell's driving school at Snetterton. In 1970 he moved into Formula Two (coming third in the European Championship) and then Colin Chapman gave him a Lotus to drive.

Due to the untimely death of Jochen Rindt he found himself Lotus team leader after only three races in Formula One. When he won the American Grand Prix at Watkins Glen at the end of the season it was only his fifth Grand Prix race and his experience of single-seat racing in Europe went back only 18 months.

He came tenth in the World Championship that year, sixth in 1971 and despite some slowish starts from the grid he had the World Title in the bag when he won the Italian Grand Prix in September 1972, his fifth Grand Prix win of the season. The first South American to win the title since Fangio, he became the world's best-known Brazilian after Pele, the footballer.

His championship-winning car, the John Player Special, designed by Maurice Phillippe, was wedge-shaped, with side radiators and used the Ford V8 engine.

Jacky Ickx

If all *grandes épreuves* were held in the rain, then the Belgian would probably have been World Champion several times over instead of runner-up on two occasions. For he is the current master of the wet track and

Emerson Fittipaldi
(Braz)

 Graham Hill
(GB)

 Jackie Stewart
(GB)

 François Cevert
(Fr)

 Denny Hulme
(NZ)

 Peter Revson
(USA)

 Jackie Ickx
(Belg)

 Mike Hailwood
(GB)

 Jean-Pierre Beltoise
(Fr)

 Chris Amon
(NZ)

monocoque', using a spaceframe reinforced by riveted sheet aluminium.

Ickx has also had considerable success in sports cars; his Le Mans victory in 1969 was in a Ford.

Chris Amon

Without a doubt the unluckiest driver in Formula One, Amon has the unenviable reputation of picking the wrong team at any given time. He has been driving in Formula One since he was a 19 year-old in 1963 and by 1973 he had amassed a long list of placings but had still to win a world championship Grand Prix.

Son of a sheep rancher, he joined his fellow New Zealander Bruce McLaren to win the Le Mans 24 Hours race of 1966 in a Ford, thereby breaking the Ferrari grip on this classic race. Ferrari charitably rewarded him by taking him into the Formula One team for 1967 but Amon saw his team leader Bandini killed at Monaco and afterwards nothing seemed to go right for the team. So in 1970 he left to lead the March team in its first year. What happened? The March developed a crop of teething troubles while Ickx began winning races for Ferrari.

For 1971 Amon moved to Matra. He won the Argentine Grand Prix, a non-championship event, but the car did not go well. Amon had to be content with fifth place in South Africa, third in Spain, fifth in

few drivers can compete with him when the spray is flying. His win in the Dutch Grand Prix at Zandvoort in 1971 is still talked about.

Ickx, a fast, fearless, but not always consistent driver, has little time for motor racing politics and particularly for drivers who agitate for ambitious safety schemes. When the Grand Prix Drivers Association backed their demands by boycotting Spa and the Nurburgring in 1970, Ickx resigned from their ranks in protest.

Born in 1945 he began on two wheels in motor-cycle trials, switching to cars for hill climb events (and turning his car over in the first that he entered). In 1965 he won the Belgian saloon car championship in a Lotus-Cortina.

He was a tank instructor in the Belgian army when Ken Tyrrell, Jackie Stewart's mentor, gave him his first chance in single seaters with a Formula Three Matra. Tyrrell then promoted him to a Formula Two Matra to drive alongside Stewart in 1967 and he won the European championship.

He made his Formula One debut that year in a Cooper, moved to Ferrari in 1968, Brabham in 1969 and then returned to Ferrari as team leader. His Formula One Ferrari, a flat 12, gave some 470 b.h.p., which made it probably the most powerful car on the grid. Designed by Mauro Forghieri, it was a 'false

France, sixth in Italy. Meanwhile, the March took Ronnie Peterson to second place in the World Championship. Typical of Amon's luck in 1972 was leading the French Grand Prix until half distance and then suffering a puncture which put him in third place.

His Matra-Simca, designed by Robert Morin, was a full monocoque with a tubular subframe in front, using the Matra V12 engine.

Graham Hill

Probably the most popular figure in motor sport and certainly the driver best known to the ordinary man and woman, Hill has a wryly dry sense of humour and is a witty speaker, much in demand as an after-dinner speech-maker and a TV personality. He is also a man of enormous determination, which has been seen throughout his career—because he was never a natural driver like Stewart.

A stockbroker's son, he started motor racing after paying £1 to drive four laps at Brands Hatch. He registered as an unemployed racing driver and drew dole money while offering his services as a mechanic to anyone who would give him an occasional drive. Eventually he settled for a job as a Lotus mechanic.

His Formula One debut was made for Lotus at Monaco in 1958 and he lost a wheel when lying fourth —but he has since won that race five times! In 1960 he

joined BRM and two years later brought them their first World Championship. In 1967 he returned to Lotus and won the championship again the following year.

Then in 1969 he suffered a terrible crash at Watkins Glen, smashing both legs. It was feared he might never walk again without a stick but sheer determination enabled him to drive again five months later. Though in pain, he drove a privately entered car in the South African Grand Prix—and finished sixth.

Though the accident and his age—he had turned 40 —meant that he had passed the peak of his career, he gained a place in the Brabham team, driving the full monocoque Ford-engined Formula One car designed by Ron Tauranac.

Hill has also driven successfully in most other formulae. When he won the Indianapolis 500 in a Lotus-Ford in 1966 he used his winnings to buy a plane in which he piloted himself between circuits. In 1972 he won the Le Mans 24 Hours race with Henri Pescarolo in a Matra-Simca.

Denny Hulme

Tough, taciturn, burly Denny Hulme, son of a New Zealand World War II Victoria Cross winner, is the most reserved man in Formula One. Born in 1936 he first raced an MG in local hill climbs, then in 1959 he

117

won a driver's scholarship to Europe, where he became a Brabham mechanic.

In 1962–3 he drove a Brabham in Formula Junior, preparing the car himself. He moved on to Formula Two, coming second to Brabham himself in the Formula Two Championship. He drove his first Grand Prix at Monaco in 1965 and finished eighth. In 1966 he was Brabham's team-mate in Formula One. Brabham won the World Championship and Hulme was fourth, but the next year he beat his boss and won the title with victories at Monaco and Nurburgring. As World Champion he broke the hearts of interviewers from popular papers by his total lack of interest in exploiting the title.

His parting from Brabham after this surprised no one; he joined his compatriot Bruce McLaren, who had won a driver's scholarship from New Zealand two years earlier and was now making his own cars. The light-hearted, highly articulate McLaren and the strong, bear-like Hulme made a good team, and he continued driving the orange cars after McLaren's death.

His Yardley McLaren Formula One car of the 'seventies was designed by Ralph Bellamy and was a full monocoque using the Ford V8 engine. He was champion of the Can-Am series in 1968 and 1970.

Mike Hailwood

He was the greatest of all motorcycle racing champions, winning nine world titles and taking the chequered flag in 75 Grands Prix and 12 TT races. But his transition from two to four wheels was a slow one.

He first essayed car racing in 1954 with a private Lotus but returned to bikes. In 1963 he tried cars again in sports car and Formula 5000 events without startling success, and was beginning to be written off as a great rider but an ordinary driver. Then in 1971 he was enlisted by John Surtees, who won seven World Championships on motorcycles himself before turning to racing and then making cars, and suddenly Hailwood's career took off. That year he came second in the Formula 5000 Championship to Australia's Frank Gardner.

When Surtees put him into the Italian Grand Prix 'Mike the Bike' led the race for much of the time and finished fourth. In 1972, in the same event, he came second, and had meanwhile taken himself to the top of the Formula Two ratings.

A bachelor with a vast collection of jazz hi-fi records, he was apparently still happier in Formula Two than in Formula One, driving the Ford-engined monocoque car with a chassis designed by 'Big John' Surtees himself. But he was beginning to pick up championship points.

Jean-Pierre Beltoise

The French hero, son of a Parisian butcher, was another motorcycle racer. He won 11 French cham-

Far left
Denis Hulme.

Left
Jean Pierre Beltoise.

Right
A March swings through the long hairpin at Brands Hatch; Spring 1972.

pionships, then began motor racing in 1963 while a mechanic at the works of the specialist car firm of René Bonnet.

Beltoise raced Formula Two and GT cars for Bonnet until a crash in the Rheims 12 hours event nearly cost him his life. He suffered arm and leg injuries which still trouble him. When he returned to work six months later he found that the Matra aero firm had taken over the Bonnet company and had built a Formula Three car. He drove it and won the French Formula Three championship.

He moved on to Formula Two and drove his Formula Two car in Formula One events in 1967, winning a race in South Africa. He won the European Formula Two Championship and became Jackie Stewart's No. 2 in the Tyrrell Matra-Ford team of 1969, and later leader of the Matra team.

But 1971 was a disastrous year for this fast, brave driver. He was suspended for several months after an accident in the Argentine 1,000 km race when Ignazio Giunti of Italy smashed into Beltoise's out-of-fuel car which he was pushing along the track. Giunti died in flames and Beltoise was held largely responsible.

For 1972 he moved to become a leader of the Marlboro BRM team, driving the Tony Southgate-designed semi-monocoque with rear tubular sub-frame and BRM V12 engine. He opened the season well with a win at Monaco, where he was never challenged after the first bend.

Ronnie Peterson

The blond blue-eyed Swede was the sensation of 1971 when he was runner-up to Stewart in the World Championship in only his second season in Formula One racing.

Born in 1944, he owned his first car at the age of eight—a 50 c.c. midget built for him by his father. He became Sweden's kart champion before buying a Tecno Formula Three car and winning the Swedish Formula Three Championship.

In 1969 the March Formula One car was on the stocks and a Formula Three car was built as a prototype. March gave Peterson a drive at Cadwell Park and he finished third. On his next outing he crashed, but March signed him to a three-year contract while he was still in hospital.

He drove through 1970, the March's debut year, without great success, for the car disappointed with weight and handling problems. But in 1971, though he never won a major race, he piled up the points with his effective though inexperienced and unpolished flat-out-from-the-start style of driving. He also survived a number of dangerous looking situations into which his rawness led him, to become European Formula Two Champion and was talked of as the obvious successor to Stewart's crown.

His March Formula One car was designed by Robin Herd with a body by Frank Costin, and used the Ford V8 engine.

119

Chapter 16

Sports Cars

Prince Henry to GT40

In tracing the origins and development of the so-called 'sports' car it would be all too simple to fall into the age-old trap of trying to decide just which were sports cars and which were not. At first a car was a car, and if one was raced or 'trialed' what was it then? Answer—nobody quite knew. Very early competition cars—those that took part in late nineteenth century sport—were no different from those that carried madame around the Bois de Boulogne for a morning spin; it was only with the arrival of Mercedes in 1900–1 that automobilists with a touch of the competitive spirit began to examine the works for possible improvements and to shed a brass lamp, a mudguard and a seat or two in the name of *le sport*. But motoring still had to wait almost a decade for a car to prove itself a true sporting vehicle, designed for touring and competition.

The First 'Sports Car'

After their successes in the Prince Henry trials, which began in 1907, Vauxhall decided not only to market a 'Prince Henry' model but to advertise it as a 'sports car'. However, this could not be claimed as an all-British 'first', for one cannot overlook some of the other cars that appeared in those competitions, particularly the Austro-Daimlers, designed by no lesser man than Ferdinand Porsche.

The Vauxhall Prince Henry prototype, with designer Laurence Pomeroy at the wheel, on an experimental run to Lulworth Cove in Dorset, 1910.

The 1914 Mercedes *Sportwagen* had six cylinders, rated 28/95 h.p. and was a direct sports car descendant of the 1908 Grand Prix car. This model was produced in series after the war ended.

The trials were an effort, sponsored by Prince Henry of Prussia, whose name they bore, to provide a form of motoring competition on the public roads that was *not* a race. They were in fact more like a present-day rally than anything else, and one of them even had part of the course set in Great Britain. Of the cars, the Austro-Daimler and the Vauxhall are by far the most interesting, and although fundamentally very different, were superficially alike in the big aggressive 'V' radiators with which they were fitted, and the rakish coachwork they carried. Porsche went for power with a massive 5.7 litre single overhead-camshaft engine, but with old-fashioned (even in those days) total-loss lubrication and with the final drive still operated by chains—a practice the Germans held on to for some time with their massive and powerful engines, since it was reliable if nothing else.

Laurence Pomeroy Sr, the Vauxhall designer, went for something much lighter and more refined and, incidentally, based on his firm's current production cars. He produced a side-valve 3 litre car which originally gave little more than 38 b.h.p. However, over the years, it was much improved and by 1913 was a 4 litre affair giving something like 75 b.h.p. at the then very high speed of 2,500 r.p.m. From this was developed Vauxhall's most illustrious car, the 30/98.

Searching for Power

It would be wrong to imagine that these were the only forebears of the sports cars which flourished in the period between the two wars. There were many notable models, particularly from continental manufacturers such as Mercedes and de Dietrich; and the British Silver Ghost Rolls-Royce and big Napiers played their part. In addition, of course, the influence of the early racing cars was profound, particularly when Peugeot introduced the twin overhead-camshaft engine to the 1912 Grand Prix scene, two years before war brought motor sport to a temporary halt. But the war did not stop the development of the sports car since the work done on engines, particularly aero engines, was to be a stimulus for design quite beyond anything that could have happened in peace-time.

The Years Between

As soon as the war was over the demand for sports cars—more for use on the road than in competition—soon flooded in to manufacturers, a demand boosted by the war experiences of many potential buyers. Much of the excitement had gone out of life when peace returned and in the frenetic 'twenties the possession of a good sports car seemed to many a way of putting that excitement back.

W. O. Bentley was early on the scene with the first car of his own manufacture—the 3 litre. He had had considerable success in the pre-war period with the French DFP for which he had been the British concessionnaire; during the war he had worked on aero engines and had been largely responsible for the introduction of the aluminium piston (which made possible a much higher engine speed, without loss of reliability). His post-war 3 litre was a big car and surprisingly the 1921 model only managed 65 b.h.p. at 3,500 r.p.m., but by 1926 the 'speed model' was up to 85 b.h.p. and could exceed 100 m.p.h. Developing alongside this car was the 30/98 Vauxhall, a direct descendant of the pre-war 'Prince Henry' and introduced in 1913.

It would be fair to say that these two cars, Bentley and Vauxhall, formed the foundation for the develop-

ment of the sports car—at any rate in Britain—and it would be difficult to prove that continental manufacturers were not also influenced by them. Later the French, largely under the influence of Bugatti, produced a new and smaller breed, and it was not until these two schools had begun to merge that the apotheosis of the sports car came about in the late 'thirties.

Golden Days of Stutz and Mercer

In America the influences on design had been very different. Motoring had started free of many of the legal restrictions that had beset Europe, and had started with a quite different conception of the motor car. It had quickly become a necessity in the opening up of the West and was all too soon accepted as part of everyday life. There had also been freedom from fuel taxation and gasoline was cheap; in consequence

engines were large and powerful—simple in design and
generally reliable. A sporting interest had quickly
sprung up, and the Vanderbilt Cup races had been a
parallel to the Gordon Bennett events in Europe. There
was, therefore, a limited demand for something very
close to what Europe was calling a 'sports car',
although the main automotive interest was in a
vehicle that could travel reliably over the still appalling
road surfaces.

The two most notable models in the 1910–7 period
were the Mercer Type 35 Raceabout and later the
Stutz Bearcat speedster. The Type 35 introduced in
1911, was conventional in terms of engineering, having
a 5 litre T-head engine producing little more than
50 b.h.p. and driving through a conventional clutch
and a three-speed gearbox. It was particularly unusual
in the matter of coachwork—or rather the lack of it;
the car was marketed with only two bucket seats and a
bolster petrol tank behind them. It had no body as
such, though it was fitted with elegant mud-wings and
a 'monocle' windscreen. Its light weight enabled it to
use very high gear ratios and to be capable of some
75 m.p.h. With various changes it lasted until about
1923, when the demand for it disappeared.

The Stutz—introduced in 1914—was similar in
appearance and indeed in conception. It managed 60
b.h.p. at a mere 1,500 r.p.m. and had its three-speed
gearbox integral with the back axle. This model, a hot
rival to the Raceabout (the term sports car was not
used in the United States until later) sold for $2,000 in
1914. Sang the Raceabout fans: 'You must be nuts to
drive a Stutz'—but it was the Stutz that went on to
race at Le Mans, and to outlast the Mercer Automobile
Company by some ten years.

The Importance of Le Mans

The decision in 1923 to hold an annual 24 hours race
at Le Mans in the Sarthe region of France was an open
challenge to all manufacturers of production sports
cars, for the regulations clearly demanded that the
entries should bear the closest possible resemblance to
cars seen in the showroom, and on the road in the
hands of ordinary owners. So the Le Mans event
became, in the period between the wars, the one great

Left
Covering the grid at this 1936
race at the Nürburgring
(Schloss Nürburg can be seen
in the background) are a
dozen BMW 2 litre cars. This
car dominated its class from
1936 to 1939 in European
sports car racing.

Above
1931; the start of the tenth TT.
Britain's oldest established
motor race, the Royal
Automobile Club Tourist
Trophy was first held in 1905.
Here Austins and small MGs
get away at the head of the line
for a Le Mans-type start.

test by which a sports car could be judged. W. O.
Bentley immediately threw himself and his firm into
the fray, and although in the first year (1923) his single
3 litre entry only managed to come in fifth he was
to win the race at the Sarthe circuit five times before
his company went out of production in 1931. The cars
developed for this race found a ready market and the
3 litre was quickly followed by a $4\frac{1}{2}$ litre and that in
turn (1929) by the first 6 cylinder Bentley, the $6\frac{1}{2}$ litre
Speed 6. Bentley's final effort (the 8 litre) was not
intended for racing; but as commercial competition
for the Continental Rolls-Royce. Vauxhall who were
absorbed by General Motors in 1925, did not pursue
the competition, although many others did. Even
those that did not compete at Le Mans and elsewhere
were all too ready to produce showroom sports cars
for a hungry market.

Among the most interesting of the non-competing
sports cars was the 3 litre Sunbeam with its twin-
overhead camshaft engine, made between 1925 and
1930, while Lagonda produced a handsome and
worthwhile 2 litre car which 'grew-up' into a $4\frac{1}{2}$ litre
(Type M45) model, which in its turn became the 1935
Le Mans winner.

New Ideas from Europe

For some years after World War I the major European makers seemed to be following Bentley's lead.
Chenard-Walcker, Lorraine, Alfa Romeo and of
course Mercedes were all producing big, high, thunder-
ing models similar in concept to the other Le Mans
competitors, the ultimate being the SSK Mercedes of
7.1 litres with supercharger, which, though never
beating the Bentley at its own game enjoyed many
competition successes and was sure to stop any small
boy (and his father) dead in their tracks if ever seen
driving down the street.

However the wind of change was blowing from both
France and Italy—strongest perhaps from the direction of Molsheim in Alsace, where an emigré Italian
by the name of Bugatti had set up his works in the
newly-returned French territory. The most individual
of all manufacturers, Bugatti produced a very wide

range of cars (36 models, but fewer than 10,000 cars!) over the years from the smallest at 1,092 c.c. up to the great 12.7 litre Bugatti Royale—one of the largest cars ever made. His 1,500 c.c. and 2.3 litre racing and sports cars brought Bugatti his greatest successes and, although by no means the fastest cars of their time in terms of outright speed, they were endowed with road-holding unsurpassed in their day and frequently unequalled even now. Bugatti was not alone—there were myriad small sports car manufacturers in France and more in Italy, many following the Bugatti lead.

R.P.M. Equals Power

To get the maximum power from these small engines it was necessary to increase considerably their ability to 'rev'. The modest engine speeds which sufficed for the large cars were inadequate for the smaller units, and high compression ratios, twin overhead camshafts and superchargers became commonplace in the sports model. Working in this field, but with much larger cars, Georges Roesch, a Swiss who had taken charge of design at the British Talbot works, was one of the great pioneers of engine design. Spurning overhead camshafts in favour of push rods and valve rockers of unique design, he produced a highly successful and interesting range of sports cars of great significance.

New Wine in Old Bottles

Many of these new engines were put into frames of a very conventional type, and indeed up to the mid-thirties there was some development but little radical change in overall design. Almost all cars still used 'cart' springs and most of the improvements were in the fields of tyre and shock-absorber design. However, by 1935–6 startling developments in this field began to be seen. These changes owed their impetus to the German entry into Grand Prix racing, where, with large sums of government money and a great deal of 'encouragement' from Adolf Hitler, the two German teams of Auto-Union and Mercedes produced some very advanced cars which swept all before them. Their thinking was quickly followed by the German BMW concern who produced first a 1½ litre and later the sophisticated Type 328 sports two-seater with the power unit developed from the earlier 2 litre, quickly leading most other manufacturers in the same direction. France soon followed this line of development; unable on financial grounds to keep pace with the Grand Prix situation they directed their expertise to the sports car field with Delahaye and the French Talbot (by then no longer connected with the British firm). Chassis developments together with the improved engines made a big advance in sports cars

Left
First Jaguar win at Le Mans, 1951. Peter Walker leads a pair of Cunninghams.

Right
This end of the line. One of today's finest sportive vehicles, the Ferrari Dino 246 GT.

Below
Small saloon car racing in the late 60s. Here Minis and Ford Anglias sweep round Copse Corner at Silverstone.

generally, the out-and-out near-racers becoming very fast indeed, and a new breed of quiet, comfortable but sportive models coming on to the market.

Although the main sports car development was continental, things were stirring in Great Britain—the last major country to enter the motor manufacturing field, due to its long-outdated laws relating to use of the highways by self-propelled vehicles. Beginning with the immortal Austin Seven and quickly followed by the MG Midget, a race of small sports·cars grew up in this country based on the small production saloons. Many of them quickly gained a deservedly bad reputation being little more than sports-type open bodies on anything but sports-type chassis and capable with a following wind of not much more than 60 m.p.h. But there were also some splendid developments—Austin, MG and Riley being among the best and the Wolseley Hornet Special among the most

controversial—and many racing cars were developed from several of these quite humble models, the most notable being the ERA out of the Riley.

The Age of the Jaguar
The industrial setbacks of World War II were more serious in some ways than those of World War I—although the technical advances were probably more numerous. Nevertheless when peace returned most manufacturers went back to making what they had made before the hostilities started. However, some brilliant new ideas were afoot, and by 1948 Jaguar had produced the XK 120 with its 3.4 litre twin o.h.c. 6 cylinder engine giving 160 b.h.p.—a massive step forward in the development of the sports car.

Then there was the Aston Martin. The company, long famous for its 1½ litre models, was bought shortly after the war by David Brown who had at the

Below
An Escort race in the
'70s, packed tight at Brands
Hatch.

same time acquired Lagonda. The firm had commissioned W. O. Bentley to design a new car and he had produced a twin o.h.c. engine of 2.6 litres (soon expanded to 3 litres) which was put in an Aston Martin chassis. This car (DB2) raced with some success at Le Mans and the Mille Miglia in 1950 and 1951.

The development of the Aston Martin, the Jaguar XK, and the products of the Ferrari company in Italy, set the pace for post-war sports car racing and development and it was only a revived interest in sports cars in America that changed the scene of today's pattern of competition.

The American Revival

From 1941 to 1946 Britain was home to a great number of American servicemen, many of whom took a keen interest in, among other things, the European sports car, for in the period between the wars the sports car was almost unknown in America except for the few imports of foreign machines by a small coterie of enthusiasts. The Duesenberg had gone out of produc-

tion and although Hollywood stimulated an interest in luxury vehicles of a 'sporting' nature, no one in their right mind would have called them sports cars.

When the servicemen returned to the United States they took this sports car enthusiasm with them (as well as a great many examples) and it is from this that the present American interest in Grand Prix and sports car racing springs. Headed in the early 'fifties by Briggs Cunningham, who built some special cars and made a real effort to succeed at Le Mans, the Americans jumped in at the deep end. Cunningham's first was a Cadillac special entered in the 1950 24 hours of Le Mans, a vehicle known to the locals as *Le Monstre*. The French were to see many more American monsters before the decade was out, as Cunningham's later cars, with big 5.4 Chrysler power-packs invaded the Sarthe region in an attempt to wrest success from the Europeans.

Curiously, the American desire to succeed at Le Mans led indirectly to the changes in racing which revived saloon car racing.

Right
Silverstone sequence during the saloon car heyday. Coming through Copse Corner a Sunbeam Rapier driven by Peter Harper is off course and gets a nose-on shunt from Cristabel Carlisle's Mini. The Mini stays on its wheels but the Rapier rolls, and is climbed all over by the lady driver. An incident enjoyed by all . . .

To go back to the beginning of the change one must look at post-war Le Mans. Firstly, there were a string of Jaguar successes, then, at long last, a victory for Aston Martin. These were all regular sports cars in the old sense of the word. Mercedes chipped in with a Grand Prix prototype but somehow seemed not to be breaking either the rules or the spirit of the rules. Then came a string of Ferrari victories still with what were recognizably sports cars under the old rules. Cunningham never won, but the American interest never waned. Ford took up the challenge and finally succeeded with the GT40 (in a 1–2–3 Le Mans victory in 1966) which was still recognizable as a road car—and indeed a number were made for everyday private use on ordinary roads.

Back to Saloons

Soon after this however the Le Mans authorities found reason to admit much less standard cars under the heading of 'prototypes' and soon enough of the cars running there bore little or no resemblance to the models seen on the public road. Concurrently with these developments came the Canadian–American series of sports car races, generally known as the Can-Am series; which, although for 'sports cars' in name, is in fact for racing cars—racing cars by any other name, or any other formula—so impractical would they be off the track.

Thus, there is a situation where the true sports car has all but ceased to exist. The Sprite goes on as does the TR6; but there are next-to-no competitions for them to race in.

As a counter-measure we have saloon car racing, in an effort to mount some events which cater for the 'same as you can buy' vehicle. In many cases, of course, they are not at all the same. Much recent racing is under 'Group Two' regulations of the international authority and, the cars are so 'wild', that apart from the general shape of the body-pressings they are almost altogether special. So we have a situation in which 'sports cars' are racing cars and saloon cars are sports cars, while on the road the sports car has ceased to exist in name and has been replaced by a closed model usually known as a 'GT' car.

But now in the early 'seventies saloon car racing is getting back to basics, and the ever-increasing development in the Group Two field, allowing so many complexities into the engineering that the fun had been engineered out of the sport, may give way to standard products on the circuit. Sparked off in Britain by a Ford Escort Mexico Challenge series dreamed up by Ford, Group One (near-standard) racing has grown, and one can see Hillman Avengers chased by Datsuns, followed by an occasional big loping American. Handicaps even it out somewhat but the spectacle is back—and the crowds, too, are beginning to be attracted once again to watch competition between their own models and those of the guy next door. Just like it used to be in the late 'fifties and 'sixties in fact, when a car's genuine characteristics could be seen in action in the hands of an expert.

129

World Champions

The first one, in 1950, was Farina. Farina the maestro, as he was called, Farina the stylist, the teacher. His long-arm style of driving was taken up eventually by all racing drivers, who hitherto hugged the wheel in the style of the 'twenties and 'thirties. Stirling Moss was one—and he brought the relaxed driving position with its easier control to the circuits of Britain.

The World Championship of Drivers was first won by Guiseppe Farina driving an Alfa Romeo 158. In the 23 Grande Epreuve seasons following that historic year a dozen other names have earned the ultimate title . . . from Argentina, Italy, Britain, Australia, United States of America, New Zealand, Austria and Brazil . . .

Alberto Ascari, Italy. World Champion 1952, 1953.

Guiseppe Farina, Italy. World Champion 1950.

John Michael Hawthorn, Great Britain. World Champion 1958.

John Arthur Brabham, Australia. World Champion 1959, 1960, 1966.

Juan Manuel Fangio, Argentine. World Champion 1951, 1954, 1955, 1956, 1957.

Philip T. Hill, United States.
World Champion 1961.

Norman Graham Hill, Great
Britain. World Champion
1962, 1968.

James Clark, Great Britain.
World Champion, 1963, 1965.

John Surtees, Great Britain.
World Champion, 1964.

Denis Clive Hulme, New
Zealand. World Champion 1967.

Karl Jochen Rindt, Austria.
World Champion 1970.

John Young Stewart, Great
Britain. World Champion
1969, 1971.

Emerson Fittipaldi, Brazil.
World Champion 1972.

Chapter 17

Formula Everything

The Melting Pot

For every Grand Prix driver who has struggled his way through to a hard-earned position in a works Formula One team, there are a hundred hopefuls on their way up through the junior formulae with an envious eye cast on his position. But the apprenticeship to competitive top-line racing is just as close-fought as Formula One and there will be but a handful of those who start the road in either Formula Three or Formula Ford actually emerging, three or four years later, as Grand Prix talent. For some the road just peters away, others just keep ploughing on, but *one* of the novices you can see at your local circuit in a single-seater is virtually bound to make it. Thus it's very worthwhile to consider the formulae in which the aces of the future are making their name.

Formula Two—the great levelling ground

Before World War II, a class for smaller engined single-seaters arose at a time when Grand Prix cars were so prohibitively priced that the only way of getting a really competitive machine was to be a member of a works team. Of course this privilege fell only to a fortunate few, but there were still private owners who wanted, and could afford, to race internationally. Limited to just 1½ litres, there were races for voiturettes all over Europe, and cars like the ERA,

Formula Three grid. In camera is an Ensign LNF3 Ford Holbay, Stan Matthews in the cockpit.

South African Jody Scheckter
in a works McLaren Formula
Two car.

designed by Peter Berthon and Humphrey Cook and
driven by Raymond Mays, provided the training
ground necessary for budding Formula One stars.

After the war this formula provided the basis of the
1½ litre supercharged Formula One, but Formula Two
(as it became known) evolved in 1947 as a 2 litre unsupercharged class, and since that day has been
altered on several occasions right up until 1972, when
it became the haven of production-based motors up to
2 litres (1,000 cylinder heads had to be made to
qualify, although for 1973 this was altered to 100
heads). The principal behind this is to ensure that costs
are kept down—although experience has shown that
race preparation of a basically production motor can
be every bit as expensive as a pure competition unit
which, being purpose built, tends to be more reliable.

Since the early 1960s, in which time we've had a 1
litre, 1.6 litre and now 2 litre Formula Two, the
spectator attraction has been realized by organizers all
over Europe. A private entry *can* go out and buy his
chassis from Brabham, March or Surtees, a private
entry *can* get competitive motors and, once in a while,
a private entry *can* beat all the top lines aces. It happened back in 1964 at Crystal Palace when an unknown Austrian by the name of Jochen Rindt turned
up with his privately owned Brabham-Ford and

wiped up all the top opposition, including Graham
Hill, Jim Clark and Denny Hulme. From that day
Rindt never looked back and subsequently went on to
lead the works Lotus team until his sad death in 1970.

Bearing in mind this great attraction of seeing the
Grand Prix drivers racing against promising newcomers, the European Trophy series was opened at the
start of 1967. This is a championship only for the 'non-
graded' drivers—anyone who hasn't scored two lots of
World Championship points the previous year. The
scoring system is on exactly the same 9–6–4–3–2–1
basis as the World Championship, but graded drivers
don't score. Thus if Jackie Stewart won a Formula
Two race he wouldn't take any points, but the driver
in second place, providing he was ungraded, would
take the nine.

In the years since this series started, Jacky Ickx,
Jean-Pierre Beltoise, Johnny Servoz-Gavin, Clay
Regazzoni, Ronnie Peterson and Mike Hailwood have
been the overall winners; proof surely that this 'race
within a race' system has been a great success.

Outside the European Trophy series (called the
European Championship for the first time in 1972)
there are always a number of non-championship events
which attract competitors. For although the works
entries from March, Lotus, Surtees, McLaren and

Brabham generally chase the Championship trail
there are plenty of privateers who get the chance to
feature in the results at these other races.

Look around the paddock at any Formula Two
meeting and you'll have seen possibly the most
cosmopolitan bunch of competitors in any current
formula. The young South African Jody Scheckter,
born 1950, in the works McLaren; Austria's Niki
Lauda, just a year older, with the STP-March; swarthy
Carlos Reutemann from Argentina; the Brambilla
brothers, Vittorio and Tino, from Italy; Australian
Tim Schenken and England's David Morgan.

From the sun-baked Enna circuit in Central Sicily to
the clouded forests which surround Sweden's Mantorp
Park, Formula Two provides spice, variety and entertainment in Europe from April to October, as well as
fulfilling a crucial role in unearthing stars of the future.

Formula Three—a springboard to success

As a general rule it may be said that regular winning in
Formula Two can be considered a passport to Grand
Prix driving, but there are the exceptional stars who
dominate Formula Three so decisively that their
inclusion in a Formula One team often comes immediately afterwards. Characterized by desperately
close (often a little too close) racing, Formula Three is
the lowest-but-one rung on the professional motor
racing ladder, where enthusiasm frequently overcomes
good judgment, where shunts are frequent and
(miraculously) injuries remarkably few!

Since 1971 the formula has catered for production
motors of up to 1,600 c.c. with their power restricted,
initially, by a 20 mm orifice on the atmospheric side of
the induction system. This meant reliability, but later
in 1971 the FIA agreed to open this up slightly up to

21.5 mm, which meant another 12–15 b.h.p. available; until then the motors were barely producing Formula Ford power figures, and made a noise to prove it. Wheel rim limits were introduced at the start of 1972, so anyone who was to win in Formula Three had to be a master at balancing everything on the limit.

With the exception of the very fast French Alpines from Dieppe, which use Renault motors, the Ford twin-cam has ruled the roost for the past couple of seasons, despite the intrusion of the occasional Alfa Romeo or BMW. But the variety of chassis manufacturers is bewildering; it ranges from the larger firms such as March, Brabham and Lotus to smaller specialist constructors like GRD and Ensign, both of whom are relatively recent additions to the Formula Three scene. Several firms also specialize in the preparation of the Ford twin-cams; Holbay, Vegantune and Novamotor being the most successful in terms of results over the last two seasons.

Right
Roger Williamson. From club saloon racing to Formula Two in two seasons. Already there's talk of Formula One.

Below
The fast French Alpines, using Renault motors, have challenged the Ford twin-cam in Formula Three.

And the talent? At the start of 1971, David Walker had spent two years in Formula Three. He was good, but progress didn't seem to bring him any closer to Formula Two. Luckily for him, he took heed of Lotus-maker Colin Chapman's counsel, and spent a third year in Formula Three, dominating the proceedings with a works Lotus and winning the coveted Shell Championship and Motor Sport Trophy. He catapulted straight into Formula One for the 1972 season as team-mate to Emerson Fittipaldi in the works John Player Specials.

In 1971 young Roger Williamson gave up club saloon racing, sold his old Ford Anglia and invested his life savings in a March 713. A promising start encouraged Leicester building contractor Tom Wheatcroft to sponsor his efforts for 1972. In an immaculately prepared GRD his mastery of the formula has been no less impressive than was Walker's during the previous season. Already talk of Formula One has been heard.

But if these appear to be isolated examples, there are plenty of others with talent bubbling over. Colin Vandervell, son of the millionaire behind the Vanwall Grand Prix cars is always near the head of the field; Michel Leclere from France has been consistently quick in the works Alpine-Renault; Mike Walker took the step down from Formula 5000 because he knew that Formula Three was more important to him, and has proved himself at the wheel of the works Ensign; his team-mate Rikki von Opel has matured into a driver of great promise, and Germany's Jochen Mass drove a works March with a speed and verve which marks him out for much greater things.

Every major international in Great Britain usually has a big Formula Three race on the supporting programme. Look closely amongst the spectators, you'll probably see one or two Formula One team managers who have strolled casually away from the paddock to size up who's showing well in this melting-pot of future, interesting, motor-racing talent.

Formula Ford and Super Vee—single-seater economy

Right at the bottom of the racing ladder, the novice who is just starting out will have to make up his mind about one thing. Is he doing it for pleasure, or does he want to establish himself as a professional racing driver? If the former is the case, then he may go saloon car racing. But almost inevitably, single-seaters are the way to go if professional racing is the ambition, which means Formula Ford in Britain, Super Vee in Europe.

Started as a cheap alternative to Formula Three by a British racing school, Formula Ford exploded across the racing scene at the end of 1967 with a speed which shook its founders to the core. There can seldom have been so much enthusiasm for one class of racing and

Left
Ronnie Peterson from Sweden, mainstay of the STP March Racing Team. He was runner-up in the championship stakes to Stewart in 1971.

Right
From Germany, Rolf Stommelen. The fast man for Porsche since '67, he has raced in Formula One regularly for several years.

Below
Peter Revson. He came to England from the States in 1963 to get racing experience, and first drove in Formula One in 1964, but continued to pilot Formula Two and Formula Three cars. He now drives for Team McLaren.

Below right
Australian Tim Schenken works for Surtees and shows great promise.

Merlyn, Lotus, Titan, Lola along with a host of smaller firms, pitched in with chassis for sale. Racing, conducted on road-based tyres, has been close and spectacular; there are plenty of races, so that the budding professionals can chase important championships and others can simply enjoy themselves. British Ford Cortina steel wheels are obligatory, tubular spaceframe chassis only are permitted and a great deal of reliance is put on easy-to-obtain production components.

The list of those who have started their careers in Formula Ford is endless. Tim Schenken, in 1972 with the works Surtees Formula One team, Emerson Fittipaldi, 1972 World Champion, and his team-mate David Walker, all pushed round the British club circuits at one time or another over the past five years, and what future champion may be currently racing in ten-lap clubbies at Snetterton?

Ease and cost of maintenance have made Formula Super Vee popular on the continent where Volkswagen components are readily available. It fulfils a similar purpose to Formula Ford, although monocoque chassis, racing wheels and racing tyres are permitted. From Austria to Finland, generously sponsored championships attract, and Volkswagen is very conscious of the publicity value of supporting both a British and European Championship with starting, travel and prize money.

Two years ago Jochen Mass was rubbing wheels round Hockenheim at the wheel of a Kaimann; Sweden's Gregor Kronegard, Britain's Tom Pryce and Austria's Helmut Hoinigg are others currently in the Super Vee limelight. Super Vee will almost inevitably throw up as much talent as both Formula Three and Formula Ford, and make its contribution to the small exclusive group of Grand Prix drivers.

The Survivors

Many were the names seen in the entry lists when motor racing fired the imaginations of pioneer sporting enthusiasts three generations ago; many were the backyard engineers whose products were entered in Paris races and others before World War I, small firms who backed their brain-child against the might of the relatively established manufacturers. Not many of them survived, and a large section whose popularity appeared to ensure lasting success disappeared also. Does anyone know what happened, for instance, to the CGV (France 1901-30), the Violet-Bogey (France 1913-4), the Christie (USA 1904-10) and a thousand others? These pictures are of some of the few who survived the rigours of early hazards . . .

Below
Mercedes-Benz. Racing proved Daimler's engine, under a number of marques, and a Benz raced in 1895. This is a Mercedes (before Daimler merged with Benz) in the 1924 Targa Florio.

Left
Sporting Ford. From 1901 when Henry drove in his first race, to today's rallying, saloon car racing (and Formula One participation), Fords have been part of the sporting scene. GT 40s at Le Mans in the mid-1960s.

Below
Renault has been famous since they began racing in 1899, the year Louis Renault started

production. The 1901 Paris-Berlin race saw this Renault first in the voiturette class.

Right
Racing commenced for Alfa (before Romeo) in 1911, a year after the company had started production in Milan. Last-but-one of the single-seater Alfa Romeos was the 158, although the company is active and successful in other branches of the sport.

Right
Fiat; started production 1899, started winning races, 1900. This monster is the S76, also known as the 'Brooklands 300 HP'. Its capacity was 28,338 c.c. and its purpose in life, record-breaking.

Below
Austin; still with us, and part of the British motorist's folklore. This is the 1922 Team Austin, lined up with Lord Austin on the right.

Index

Numbers in italics refer to illustrations

Acknowledgments

The author and publisher are deeply indebted to those organizations listed below for their help in making illustrations available for this book:

Alfa Romeo, American Motors Corporation, Aston Martin, Automobile Association, BMW, British Leyland, British Petroleum, Chrysler UK, Citroën, Daimler-Benz, Ferrari, Fiat, Firestone, Ford of Britain, Ford Motor Company Dearborn, General Motors, Goodyear, Indianapolis Motor Speedway, Lancia, Opel, Peugeot, Pirelli, Renault, Shell, Vauxhall.

With the exception of those detailed below all the illustrations come from Peter Roberts' Collection

Autocar: 20, 26, 40–1, 93, 130; Pete Biro: 64–5, 69, 73; Central Press Photos Ltd: 104–5; Gero Hoscheck: 70; Louis Klementaski: 54, 57, 89; London Art Tech: front jacket, 50–1, 55, 59, 95, 112–4, 116–8, 128, 130, 131, 134, 136, 137; T.A.S.O. Mathieson: 32, 33, 56, 67, 79; National Motor Museum: jacket back flap, 18–9; Sport & General Press Agency: 131; Stanbury Foley on behalf of John Player: 115; Les Thacker: 110–1.